D1044100

HYMNS FOR TODAY

Also Available in the For Today Series:

HYMNS
FOR TODAY

Brian Wren

WESTMINSTER
JOHN KNOX PRESS
LOUISVILLE · KENTUCKY

For Anna, Helen, and Laurence Wareing
Friends Indeed

© 2009 Brian Wren

First edition
Published by Westminster John Knox Press
Louisville, Kentucky

09 10 11 12 13 14 15 16 17 18—10 9 8 7 6 5 4 3 2 1

All rights reserved. No part of this book may be reproduced or transmitted in any form or by any means, electronic or mechanical, including photocopying, recording, or by any information storage or retrieval system, without permission in writing from the publisher. For information, address Westminster John Knox Press, 100 Witherspoon Street, Louisville, Kentucky 40202-1396. Or contact us online at www.wjkbooks.com.

Scripture quotations from the New Revised Standard Version of the Bible are copyright © 1989 by the Division of Christian Education of the National Council of the Churches of Christ in the U.S.A. and are used by permission.

Scripture quotations marked NEB are taken from *The New English Bible*, © The Delegates of the Oxford University Press and The Syndics of the Cambridge University Press, 1961, 1970. Used by permission.

Book design by Sharon Adams
Cover design by Eric Walljasper, Minneapolis, MN

Library of Congress Cataloging-in-Publication Data
Wren, Brian A.
  Hymns for today / Brian Wren.
    p. cm. — (For today series)
  Includes bibliographical references and index.
  ISBN 978-0-664-22934-4 (alk. paper)
  1. Hymns, English—20th century—History and criticism. 2. Hymns, English—21st century—History and criticism. 3. Hymns, English—Texts. I. Title.
  BV312.W64   2009
  264'.23—dc22   2009002874

PRINTED IN THE UNITED STATES OF AMERICA

♾ The paper used in this publication meets the minimum requirements of the American National Standard for Information Sciences—Permanence of Paper for Printed Library Materials, ANSI Z39.48-1992.

Westminster John Knox Press advocates the responsible use of our natural resources. The text paper of this book is made from 30% post-consumer waste.

Contents

Series Introduction

*T*he For Today series is intended to provide reliable and accessible resources for study of important biblical texts, theological documents, and Christian practices. The series is written by experts who are committed to making the results of their studies available to those with no particular biblical or theological training. The goal is to provide an engaging means to study texts and practices that are familiar to laity in churches. The authors are all committed to the importance of their topics and to communicating the significance of their understandings to a wide audience. The emphasis is not only on what these subjects have meant in the past but also on their value in the present—"For Today."

Our hope is that the books in this series will find eager readers in churches, particularly in the context of education classes. The authors are educators and pastors who wish to engage church laity in the issues raised by their topics. They seek to provide guidance for learning, for nurture, and for growth in Christian experience.

We hope the books in this series will be important resources to enhance Christian faith and life.

The Publisher

Acknowledgments

*T*he following individuals and entities have kindly given permission for copyrighted texts to be quoted in this book.

Ronald Cole-Turner
John Brownlow Geyer
Jean Janzen
Helen Laughton
James K. Manley
Ruth Micklem
David Pitt-Watson
Marjean Postlethwaite
The Archdiocese of Philadelphia
Augsburg Fortress, 100 South Fifth Street, Suite 600, Minneapolis, MN 55402. www.augsburgfortress.org
Concordia Publishing House, 3558 S. Jefferson, St. Louis, MO 63118. www.cph.org
The Copyright Company (on behalf of the United Methodist Publishing House), P.O. Box 128139. Nashville, TN 37212-8139. www.thecopyrightco.com
G.I.A. Publications Inc., 7404 S. Mason Ave., Chicago, IL 60638-3438. www.giamusic.com, (800) 442-1358
Hope Publishing Company, 380 South Main Place, Carol Stream, IL 60188. www.hopepublishing.com
Medical Mission Sisters, 77 Sherman Street, Hartford, CT 06105. www.medicalmissionsisters.org
Music Services, Inc., 5409 Maryland Way, #200, Brentwood, TN 37027. www.musicservices.org

Oregon Catholic Press, 5536 N.E. Hassalo St., Portland, OR 97213-3638. www.ocp.org

Oxford University Press, Great Clarendon Street, Oxford OX2 6D, England – UK. www.oup.co.uk/rights

Selah Publishing Co., Inc., 4055 Cloverlea St., P.O. Box 98066, Pittsburgh, PA 15277. www.selahpub.com

1

Hymns?—For Today?

*G*ive me a moment of your time if "hymns" suggests boring words and old-fashioned music and if *Hymns for Today* sounds like *Dinosaurs for Today.*

Give me a moment of your time if hymns are a mainly musical experience, or if you encounter hymns as words dissected between staffs of music.

And if you came to Christian faith singing songs in youth events or contemporary worship and find yourself in a seminary, church, or denomination that uses a hardbound book called a *hymnal,* give me a moment of your time.

I hope to show that many hymns are poems worth speaking, hearing, and praying in worship *even if you never sing them*— and, of course, if you do.

Hymns are poems. Some are good poems. Consider this description of the crucifixion of Jesus by Isaac Watts (1674– 1748). If you've only sung it, try speaking it slowly aloud:

> See, from his head, his hands, his feet,
>   sorrow and love flow mingled down.
> Did e'er such love and sorrow meet,
>   or thorns compose so rich a crown?

The words are simple, but skillfully arranged. Looking at Jesus' head, hands, and feet, we are invited to see, not blood and water, but their deeper meaning as "sorrow and love," a phrase that balances the stanza when the next line puts it in reverse order. Thorn branches mockingly twisted by Roman soldiers become an artwork—a *composition*—that shows the majesty of suffering love.[1]

As with other types of poetry, a hymn poem can sometimes express something hard to say as memorably in prose. In a hymn on the resurrection, Thomas Troeger introduces a hard-nosed Thomas for whom the only realities are those he can smell, touch, and see—realities brutally evident at a Roman crucifixion:

> These things did Thomas count as real:
> the warmth of blood, the chill of steel,
> the grain of wood, the heft of stone,
> the last frail twitch of flesh and bone.

Though Thomas has sight, his mind-set blinds him to anything beyond his measurable world of "fact." Mentally sightless, he has to sense resurrection through his fingertips:

> His reasoned certainties denied
> that one could live when one had died,
> until his fingers read like braille
> the markings of the spear and nail.[2]

In examples like these, hymn verses rise to the level of poetry. What else is a line like "sorrow and love flow mingled down"? Where else is "nail" paired so tellingly with "braille"?

In chapters that follow I shall look at a number of hymn poems and explore their insights into Christian faith. But first, some brief definitions and explanations.

In form, a hymn lyric is a sequence of speech units, each with the same line length, speech rhythms, and—if the hymn is rhymed—the same rhyme scheme.[3] To distinguish them from other kinds of verse, such identical units are usually called *stanzas*. Two of Thomas Troeger's hymn stanzas are quoted above.

Part of the abiding appeal of hymns is that their stanzas can all be sung to the same tune. To a listener, a hymn sung by an average congregation may sound boring because of the sameness of its repeated tune. To an average singer in that congregation, the repeated tune makes the hymn easier to learn and sing.

A hymn's speech pattern is its *poetic meter.*[4] This has two components: the number of syllables per line and their speech rhythm. For example, "The King of love my Shepherd is" has eight syllables. So does "Glorious things of thee are spoken." But their speech rhythms differ. The first has a rhythm called iambic:

The *King* of *love* my *Shep*-herd *is.*

The second has a speech rhythm known as trochaic:

Glo-rious *things* of *thee* are *spo*-ken.[5]

Since the 1950s there has been a hymn renaissance—a remarkable flowering of English-language hymnody. Music publishers and denominational hymnals have published hundreds of new hymns. New hymns and hymnals continue to appear. In today's worship music marketplace, hymn singing is now a niche activity. But it's quite a large niche.

Limits and Choices

This book has no music. Not everyone reads music, and in a short book like this there's no room to print it. So only the words of hymns will appear. Yet music is their *hidden dimension.* If your church sings from a hymnal published during the past twenty years you will probably have sung one or more of the hymns quoted. Reading and hearing the words may trigger memories of their tunes.

My sources are hymns written and published since the 1960s. Many hymns from earlier centuries continue to be hymns for today in the sense that we still sing them. We sing them, presumably, because they continue to express our faith. But to include them in this book would obscure the importance of the hymn renaissance, increase the pool of choices from a few hundred to several thousand, turn a survey into an encyclopedia, and entail a host of value judgments hard to make and defend. So "for today" here means "from the very recent past." I shall draw on English-language hymns written and published since the mid-twentieth century and show how they express Christian faith anew or traditional themes in fresh ways. For comparison I'll high-light one "classic" hymn per chapter. Because my own hymns are part of the hymn renaissance and have been widely published, I shall draw on some of them—I hope not too many.

To gather material for this book I surveyed 250 hymns written since 1950 and published between 1983 and 2007 in twenty-three denominational hymnals (including supplemental hymnals) in the U.K., U.S.A, Canada, Australia, and New Zealand. Denominational hymnals can't tell us what people actually sing. But they are a more reliable indicator than commercial compilations and single-author collections because they are sung from more widely. Denominational hymnals in the U.K., Canada, Australia, and the U.S.A. make differ-ent selections on some theological themes, differing both from one another and over time—not to mention their widely different choices in music. So I hope the hymns quoted will introduce readers to worth-while hymns from sources beyond their denomination or region. To save space and to highlight particularly eloquent portions, most quota-tions are partial—but complete texts are accessible by first-line search online and/or through their footnoted copyright information.

Because 250 hymns are too many to deal with, I slimmed the source list.[6] To mitigate my biases, I've drawn on the most widely published authors, plus some I think we'll hear more of. I have chosen texts not only for their popularity when sung, but also for their eloquence when read or spoken.

When the hymn renaissance began, entryways into hymn writing were far more open to men than to women. So the great majority of my source texts are by male authors. By the end of my hymnal source time frame, female hymn-poets were becoming more prominent and more published. Mary Louise Bringle, Ruth Duck, Sylvia Dunstan, Gracia Grindal, Jane Parker Huber, Jean Janzen, Shirley Murray, Joy Patter-son, and Miriam Therese Winter are leading voices—and role models. Madeleine Forell Marshall's translations bring classic sources alive in fresh and fruitful ways.

This book is about hymns. Unlike chants and choruses, hymns typically express more than one idea. Many chants and choruses pub-lished since the 1960s deserve a significant place in worship but don't belong in this book. I have prioritized English-language hymns, plus a few popular translations. Because I focus on original hymn writing, I have not used many psalm and Scripture paraphrases.

Chapters 2 through 7 explore what these hymns say and how they say it. Chapter 8 is a selection printed in full for devotion, discussion, and worship.

The book concludes with notes, with hymnal sources and permission credits, and suggestions for further reading. As with other books in this series, this information is there for those who want it, without hindering an enjoyable read.

To Do and Discuss

1. Write a news story or character report on "Doubting Thomas" by putting Thomas Troeger's poem (pp. 2 and 106) into prose. What do you discover?
2. From different age groups, find five people who like hymns and five who do not. Find out why. Choose one or two hymns in chapter 8 and read them aloud to each of the ten people. How do they respond?
3. In "traditional" and (if possible) "contemporary" worship, speak or quote a hymn from chapter 8 as a prayer or meditation. *Copy it only if you get prior permission.*

Jesus

For us baptized, for us he bore
his holy fast and hungered sore,
for us temptation sharp he knew;
for us the tempter overthrew.

For us he prayed; for us he taught;
for us his daily works he wrought;
by words and signs and actions thus
still seeking not himself, but us.

For us to wicked men betrayed,
scourged, mocked, in purple robe arrayed,
he bore the shameful cross and death,
for us at length gave up his breath.

For us he rose from death again;
for us he went on high to reign;
for us he sent his Spirit here
to guide, to strengthen, and to cheer.

—From "O Love, How Deep, How Broad, How
High" (fifteenth-century Latin hymn,
trans. Benjamin Webb, 1854)

Christ—Risen

We begin with Jesus of Nazareth—to Christians Jesus *Christ*,
God's chosen one. Recent hymnals increase our opportunities

to sing about his life and work. But Christian faith begins with resurrection. Without the conviction that "for us he rose from death again" in the hymn above, and before that conviction took root, Jesus of Nazareth was only one in a long line of Jewish rebels executed by the Roman state. The public torture and humiliation of crucifixion was the standard imperial response to any subversive threat. That the Jesus movement was nonviolent didn't make it less threatening.

For people in Jesus' time, the shame of being hung naked in public was repulsive. It was as shocking as the agony of crucifixion. To most people, Jew or Gentile, the idea that a criminal crucified naked could be God's chosen liberator was a contradiction. From Paul the apostle onward, believers live with that contradiction—or paradox. In the words of Sylvia Dunstan:

> You, Lord, are both Lamb and Shepherd.
> You, Lord, are both prince and slave.
> You, peace-maker and sword-bringer
>   of the way you took and gave.
> You, the everlasting instant;
> You, whom we both scorn and crave.
>
> Clothed in light upon the mountain,
> stripped of might upon the cross,
> shining in eternal glory,
>   beggar'd by a soldier's toss,
> You, the everlasting instant;
> You who are both gift and cost.[1]

Hymns don't discuss faith. They express it. But whether discussed or expressed, Christ's resurrection is more than a past happening. It has consequences and effects from personal to cosmic. In a widely published hymn, John Geyer pictures Christ winning a wrestling match with death, on our behalf:

> We know that Christ is raised and dies no more.
> Embraced by futile death, he broke its hold,
> and our despair he turned to blazing joy.
>   Alleluia!

Alive in the church, Christ's risen presence is a sign of cosmic renewal:

> A new creation comes to life and grows
> as Christ's new body takes on flesh and blood.
> The universe, restored and whole, will sing:
> Alleluia![2]

Christ's risen presence brings possibility, even where hope has been crushed. Jesus was a Jewish male, but "Christ" names the unbounded power of his life in both genders everywhere:

> Christ is alive! No longer bound
> to distant years in Palestine,
> but saving, healing, here and now,
> and touching every place and time.
>
> In every insult, rift and war,
> where color, scorn or wealth divide,
> Christ suffers still, yet loves the more,
> and lives, where even hope has died.
>
> Women and men, in age and youth,
> can feel the Spirit, hear the call,
> and find the way, the life, the truth,
> revealed in Jesus, freed for all.[3]

Christ—Crucified

Resurrection gives divine meaning to crucifixion. Here is Dan Damon, recasting the ancient metaphor of "Christ the King" to negate hierarchical glory and power:

> Eternal Christ, you rule,
> keeping company with pain;
> enduring ridicule,
> rejected, still you reign.
>
> Eternal Christ, you rule
> speaking pardon from the cross;

> forgiving pounding nails;
> death did its worst and lost.[4]

W. H. Vanstone takes the same metaphor and rejects it. He lists a variety of divine gifts, open for all to see, then contrasts them with their hidden costs:

> Morning glory, starlit sky,
>   soaring music, scholar's truth,
>   flight of swallows, autumn leaves,
>   memory's treasure, grace of youth:
>   Open are the gifts of God,
>   gifts of love to mind and sense;
>   hidden is love's agony,
> love's endeavor, love's expense.

In a series of cascading images God's love flows through Jesus:

> Love that gives, gives ever more,
>   gives with zeal, with eager hands,
>   spares not, keeps not, all outpours,
>   ventures all, its all expends.

Amen!—though these words also need the advertiser's warning, "Divine Driver, closed course. Do not imitate." This degree of self-giving is God's alone. We cannot do it, and should not misuse Vanstone's words to justify servitude, savior-complex burnout, or dependent devotion.

The hymn now draws its striking conclusion:

> *Therefore* he who shows us God
>   helpless hangs upon the tree;
>   and the nails and crown of thorns
>   tell of what God's love must be.

"Here is God," not a monarch "throned in easy state to reign," but majesty displayed in suffering and shame—and again, with emphatic repetition:

Here is God, whose arms of love
aching, spent, the world sustain.[5]

A third hymn on the crucifixion is old, but only recently in hymnals. It comes from the oral song creation of black American slaves, and has one of the most sublime melodic lines in Christian song. It begins on a low note, asking:

Were you there when they crucified my Lord?

Then again, three tones higher:

Were you there when they crucified my Lord?

The next line begins another three tones higher, as a sigh that soars by a fourth, then falls, and steps, trembling, down:

Oh, O-oh, Oh . . . sometimes it causes me
to tremble,   tremble,   tremble.

The song then returns to a melodic variation of its beginning:

Were you there when they crucified my Lord?

Succeeding questions lead us through the drama: "Were you there when they nailed him to the tree? . . . when the sun refused to shine? . . . when they pierced him in the side? . . . when they laid him in the tomb?"[6]

This is a song to approach with care. The first singers were slaves, for whom Jesus was "*my* Lord." Who, for them, were "*they*"? Who are "they" today? What if "we" are someone else's "they"?

Jesus—Birth

As traditions about Jesus were memorized and handed down, his birth and lifework were also reinterpreted in light of his resurrection. His birth fulfills his people's long-held hopes, but with global implications:

The prophets spoke of mercy,
of freedom and release;
God shall fulfill the promise
to bring [God's] people peace.[7]

All earth is waiting to see the Promised One,
and open furrows await the seed of God.
All the world, bound and struggling, seeks true liberty;
it cries out for justice and searches for the truth . . .

For Christ lives in all Christians and comes to us now,
with peace and with justice to bring us liberty.[8]

"Christ . . . comes . . . with peace and with justice." This sounds a
new note in Christian song. Like all hymnody, the hymn renaissance
responds to its contexts, which include global poverty, the cruelties
of total war, political oppression, and the contested meanings and
mechanisms of market forces, financial systems, and corporate powers. So it is not surprising to find Jesus hailed as the embodiment of
God's peaceful justice. Miriam Therese Winter and Timothy Dudley-
Smith do so by versifying pregnant Mary's song of anticipation (the
Magnificat) in Luke 1:46–55, itself modeled on Hannah's song in 1
Samuel 2:1–10.[9] They give us a rare opportunity of observing how
two gifted hymn writers handle the same Scripture source.

Casting Scripture in English verse entails choices of nouns, verbs,
speech rhythms, and line lengths. In Luke's Gospel, Mary begins by
praising God for looking favorably on her, and for doing great things.
Our authors here express similar thoughts in different poetic meters:

My soul gives glory to my God.
My heart pours out its praise . . .
All people will declare me blessed,
and blessings they shall claim.[10] (Winter)

Tell out, my soul, the greatness of the Lord!
Unnumbered blessings give my spirit voice;
tender to me the promise of his word;
in God my Savior shall my heart rejoice.[11]
(Dudley-Smith)

Thereafter, the hymns diverge somewhat. At the heart of her song, using mostly active verbs, Mary prefigures the way God's acts in Jesus will upend the world's standards and power relationships. The New English Bible reads:

> The arrogant of heart and mind [God] has put to rout,
> he has brought down monarchs from their thrones,
>   but the humble have been lifted high.
> The hungry he has satisfied with good things,
>   the rich sent empty away.
>   (Luke 1:51–53)

Miriam Therese Winter renders this in short lines of between eight and six syllables:

> Love casts the mighty from their thrones,
>   promotes the insecure,
> leaves hungry spirits satisfied,
>   the rich seem suddenly poor.

Winter's meter enables her to be vigorous and direct. The first two lines are quite close to the source. But "leaves hungry *spirits* satisfied" turns the emphasis away from bodily hunger, while "the rich *seem* suddenly poor" considerably softens "the rich sent empty away" (emphasis mine).

Timothy Dudley-Smith begins with a direct quotation from the New English Bible—"Tell out, my soul, the greatness of the Lord." When he wrote these words he did not regard himself as a hymn writer. But recognizing the sentence as a poetic unit, he used it to begin a poem. Editors of an upcoming hymnal recognized it as a fine new hymn. It became the first of many from this author, and one of his most widely published. From this opening the hymn unfolds in flowing ten-syllable lines. Each of its four stanzas begins with the same trumpet call: "Tell out, my soul, the greatness of the Lord! . . . the greatness of his Name! . . . the greatness of his might! . . . the glories of his word!" He renders Luke 1:46–53 thus:

> Tell out, my soul, the greatness of his might!
> Powers and dominions lay their glory by.

Proud hearts and stubborn wills are put to flight,
the hungry fed, the humble lifted high.

The repeated trumpet call gives the hymn its strength, while "powers and dominions" helpfully widens the meaning of the New English Bible's "monarchs." The downside is a shift to passive verbs ("are put to flight . . . [are] fed . . . [are] lifted") and a move from the powers being cast down to what sounds like their willing departure ("lay their glory by"). I sing both hymns gladly, aware that their poetic meter closes some possibilities and opens others, and because no one hymn can say everything.

Jesus—Ministry

Crowds flocked to John the Baptizer, seeking God's forgiveness for their sins through baptism in the Jordan River. The biblical view is that Jesus walked so closely with God that he did not need forgiveness. Instead, in Fred Pratt Green's hymn,

> He came to share repentance
> with all who mourn their sins,
> to speak the vital sentence
> with which good news begins.[12]

In a human courtroom, the judge's sentence follows a guilty verdict, and delivers punishment. In Jesus, the divine sentence is "vital"— essential and life-giving—and signals the nature and direction of his ministry. A key element was healing. His healings were often experienced as the expulsion of demonic powers, as in Thomas H. Troeger's vivid portrayal of Mark 1:23–27:

> "Silence! Frenzied, unclean spirit,"
> cried God's healing, holy One.
> "Cease your ranting! Flesh can't bear it.
> Flee as night before the sun."
> At Christ's voice the demon trembled,
> from its victim madly rushed,
> while the crowd that was assembled
> stood in wonder, stunned and hushed.[13]

At the climax of Jesus' ministry, Fred Pratt Green takes us into the
Last Supper. He holds together cross and resurrection, and the con-
nection between Christ's service and ours:

> An upper room did our Lord prepare
>   for those he loved until the end:
> and his disciples still gather there,
>   to celebrate their risen Friend.
>
> A lasting gift Jesus gave his own,
>   to share his bread, his loving cup.
> Whatever burdens may bow us down,
>   he by his cross shall lift us up.
>
> And after supper he washed their feet,
>   for service, too, is sacrament.
> In him our joy shall be made complete
>   sent out to serve, as he was sent.[14]

One of my hymns gives a panoramic view of Jesus' work, seen
through the lens of his remarkable encounters with women:

> Woman in the crowd, creeping up behind,
> touching is allowed: seek and you will find!
>
> Woman at the well, question the Messiah;
> find your friends and tell: drink your heart's desire!
>
> Woman at the feast, let the righteous stare;
> come and go in peace; love him with your hair!
>
> Women on the road, from your sickness freed,
> witness and provide, joining word and deed:
>
> Women on the hill, stand when men have fled;
> Christ needs loving still, though your hope is dead.
>
> Women in the dawn, care and spices bring,
> earliest to mourn, earliest to sing!

Come and join the song, women, children, men.
Jesus makes us free to live again![15]

Perhaps the most famous recent panoramic hymn is Sydney Carter's "Lord of the Dance," which reinterprets a medieval carol set to a sprightly adaptation of a nineteenth-century American Shaker tune. The first two stanzas read:

> I danced in the morning when the world was begun,
>> And I danced in the moon and the stars and the sun,
> And I came down from heaven and I danced on the earth;
>> At Bethlehem I had my birth.

> I danced for the scribe and the Pharisee,
>> But they would not dance and they would not follow me;
> I danced for the fishermen, for James and John;
>> They came to me and the dance went on.

The third stanza raises an important question: "I danced on the Sabbath when I cured the lame, / The holy people said it was a shame" is accurate enough, but "*They* whipped and *they* stripped and *they* hung me high; And *they* left me there on a cross to die" (emphasis mine) perpetuates the pernicious belief that the Jews killed Jesus. Though the leaders of Jesus' people may have wanted him dead, death by crucifixion was a Roman prerogative, and Jewish people everywhere must not be blamed for the decisions of first-century Jewish authorities. That the Jews killed Jesus is a genocidal myth, and Carter's fine hymn here needs amendment or this stanza's omission. The hymn concludes as Christ dances on into the world and into our lives:

> They buried my body and they thought I'd gone,
> But I am the dance and I still go on.

> They cut me down and I leapt up high,
>> I am the life that'll never, never die;
> I'll live in you if you'll live in me;
>> I am the Lord of the Dance, said he.

> **Dance, then, wherever you may be;**
> **I am the Lord of the Dance, said he.**
> **And I'll lead you all wherever you may be,**
> **And I'll lead you all in the dance, said he.**[16]

To conclude this chapter, John Bell and Graham Maule ask a Christmas question that evokes the continuing unexpectedness of Jesus:

> Who would think that what was needed
> to transform and save the earth
> might not be a plan or army,
> proud in purpose, proved in worth?
> Who would think, despite derision,
> that a child should lead the way?
> God surprises earth with heaven,
> coming here on Christmas Day.[17]

To Do and Discuss

1. "Jesus was a Jewish male but 'Christ' names the unbounded power of his life in both genders everywhere" (p. 8). How can churches show that they believe this?
2. How does Christ meet you in women, men, and children? in strangers? in outcasts? in people of different languages, cultures, and faiths? in people who are poor? in homeless people? in enemies?
3. Consider the comment on "Were you there when they crucified my Lord?" on p. 20: "The first singers were slaves, for whom Jesus was "*my* Lord." Who, for them, were "*they*"? Who might "they" be today? What if "we" are someone else's "they"?
4. In light of the discussion of "Lord of the Dance" on p. 15, how should Christians behave toward Jews?
5. Compare how Timothy Dudley-Smith and Miriam Therese Winter versify Mary's song (pp. 11–13). As an exploration—for fun, not competition—try versifying Anna's story in Luke 2:36–38, with rhyme or without.

3

Spirit

Come, Holy Ghost, our souls inspire,
And lighten with celestial fire;
Thou the anointing Spirit art,
Who dost Thy sevenfold gifts impart.

Thy blessèd unction[1] from above
Is comfort, life, and fire of love;
Enable with perpetual light
The dullness of our blinded sight.

Anoint and cheer our soilèd face
With the abundance of Thy grace;
Keep far our foes, give peace at home;
Where Thou art Guide, no ill can come.

Teach us to know the Father, Son,
And Thee, of both, to be but One;
That through the ages all along
This may be our endless song:

> **Praise to Thy eternal merit,**
> **Father, Son, and Holy Spirit.[2]**

—Latin hymn "Veni Creator Spiritus,"
approx. date AD 800, attributed to Rhabanus
Maurus, Archbishop of Mainz; English version by
John Cosin, *Collection of Private Devotions in
the Practice of the Ancient Church*, 1627

*I*n Acts, chapter 2, the outpouring of the Holy Spirit fulfills Joel's prophecy and is the risen Christ's gift to the company of believers:

> Filled with the Spirit's power with one accord
> the infant church confessed its risen Lord . . .
> Like wind and fire with life among us move,
> till we are known as Christ's, and Christians prove.[3]

Thomas Troeger urges the Spirit to revive the church today:

> Wind who makes all winds that blow—
> gusts that bend the saplings low,
> gales that heave the sea in waves,
> stirrings in the mind's deep caves—
> aim your breath with steady power
> on your church, this day, this hour.
> Raise, renew the life we've lost,
> Spirit God of Pentecost.[4]

Like Rhabanus Maurus, Carl P. Daw Jr. prays "Come, Holy Spirit," (instead of the nowadays misleading "Ghost"), neatly describes the Spirit as both "gift" and "sign," and deploys Scriptural images to depict an outward-looking, loving community:

> Like the murmur of the dove's song,
> like the challenge of her flight,
> like the vigor of the wind's rush,
> like the new flame's eager might:
> come, Holy Spirit, come.
>
> To the members of Christ's Body,
> to the branches of the Vine,
> to the Church in faith assembled,
> to her midst as gift and sign:
> come, Holy Spirit, come.
>
> With the healing of division,
> with the ceaseless voice of prayer,

with the power of love and witness,
with the peace beyond compare:
come, Holy Spirit, come.[5]

Copyright © 1982 by Hope Publishing Company, Carol Stream, IL 60188. All rights reserved. Used by permission.

Within the context of a faith community, we meet the Spirit's love to each one of us and can liken it to the best in human relationships:

Like a mother you enfold me,
    hold my life within your own,
    feed me with your very body,
form me of your flesh and bone

Like a father you protect me,
    teach me the discerning eye,
    hoist me up upon your shoulder,
let me see the world from high.

Friend and lover, in your closeness
    I am known and held and blessed:
    in your promise is my comfort,
in your presence I may rest.

Loving Spirit, loving Spirit,
    you have chosen me to be —
    you have drawn me to your wonder,
you have set your sign on me.[6]

Cosmic and Historical

At Pentecost, Christ's birthday gift to the company of believers is a "wind's rush" (Daw) from the "wind who makes all winds that blow" (Troeger), the divine Spirit who creates the cosmos and ranges through it. In the words of Iona Community members John Bell and Graham Maule:

She sits like a bird, brooding on the waters,
    hovering on the chaos of the world's first day;

she sighs and she sings, mothering creation,
    waiting to give birth to all the Word will say.

She wings over earth, resting where she wishes,
    lighting close at hand or soaring through the skies;
she nests in the womb, welcoming each wonder,
    nourishing potential hidden to our eyes . . .

For she is the Spirit, one with God in essence,
    gifted by the Savior in eternal love;
and she is the key opening the scriptures,
    enemy of apathy and heavenly dove.[7]

Besides "mothering creation," the Spirit "wings over earth, resting where she wishes." Jim Manley connects these themes and looks into the future, affirming that the Spirit's work is far from finished:

You moved on the waters.
    You called to the deep.
Then you coaxed up the mountains
    from the valleys of sleep . . .

You swept through the desert,
    you stung with the sand,
and you gifted your people
    with a law and a land,
and when they were blinded
    with their idols and lies,
then you spoke through your prophets
    to open their eyes.

You sang in a stable,
    you cried from a hill,
then you whispered in silence
    when the whole world was still,
and down in the city
    you called once again,
when you blew through your people
    on the rush of the wind.

You call from tomorrow.
You break ancient schemes.
From the bondage of sorrow
    the captives dream dreams.
Our women see visions.
Our men clear their eyes.
With bold new decisions
    your people arise.[8]

The Spirit's power is promised to believing communities, but never confined to them:

When believers break the bread,
when a hungry child is fed,
    praise the love that Christ revealed,
    living, working, in our world.

Still the Spirit gives us light,
seeing wrong and setting right:
    God in Christ has come to stay.
    Live tomorrow's life today!

When a stranger's not alone,
where the homeless find a home,
    praise the love that Christ revealed,
    living, working, in our world.[9]

The above hymns have a varied vocabulary. The Spirit is God's breath or wind hovering birdlike over primeval waters (Gen. 1:2), resurrecting a lifeless people (Ezek. 37), breathed upon disciples by the risen Christ (John 20:22), and rushing upon them at Pentecost (Acts 2:2). So the Spirit can be encountered as gusts of wind, gales heaving a stormy sea, or a hot dry desert wind that blows stinging sand.

The Spirit is also the "fire" promised by John the Baptizer (Matt. 3:11; Luke 3:16), a promise fulfilled by firelike tongues that give extraordinary powers of speech (Acts 2:3–4). The New Testament image of "dove" (Matt. 3:16; Mark 1:10; Luke 3:22; John 1:32) allows us to hear the Spirit as the murmur of dove-song and the wing beats of its flight. From Genesis 1:2 comes the image of the Spirit as a female bird that hovers over primeval waters and wings across the earth, alighting and soaring at will.

The Spirit is the mother of creation, who gives birth to what the Word has spoken. She gives believers life, love, peace, and the power to love and witness, and is the key that opens the Scriptures. The Spirit sighs, sings, speaks through prophets, and whispers by the cross. She stirs sorrowing captives to dream of freedom and breaks age-old systems (schemes). The Spirit renews, raises the church to new life, gives light, exposes wrong, puts wrong things right, gives new vision, inspires bold decisions, calls to us from God's tomorrow, and inspires us to live tomorrow's life today.

Like their predecessors, today's hymnists continue to draw on old tradition. In my final selection, Jean Janzen gives us a new hymn based on a twelfth-century church leader, Hildegard of Bingen:

> O Holy Spirit, root of life,
> creator, cleanser of all things,
> anoint our wounds, awaken us
> with lustrous movement of your wings.
>
> Eternal vigor, Saving One,
> you free us by your living Word,
> becoming flesh to wear our pain,
> and all creation is restored.
>
> O holy Wisdom, soaring power,
> encompass us with wings unfurled,
> and carry us, encircling all,
> above, below, and through the world.[10]

Copyright © 1991 by Jean Janzen (admin. by Augsburg Fortress). All rights reserved. Used by permission.

To Do and Discuss

1. Someone has said that Christians believe in the Holy Spirit either too little or too much. What's your opinion and why?

2. Have you ever looked back and realized that the Holy Spirit had been at work? If so, how?
3. How has the Holy Spirit met us? Through sudden inspiration? In church budgeting? Speaking in tongues? Gentle nudging? Other people's insights, rebuke, kindness, or praise?

4

Church

Christ, from whom all blessings flow,
perfecting the saints below,
hear us, who thy nature share,
who thy mystic body are.

Move and actuate and guide;
divers[e] gifts to each divide;
Placed according to thy will,
let us all our work fulfill.

Sweetly may we all agree,
touched with loving sympathy,
kindly for each other care;
every member feel its share.

Many are we now, and one,
we who Jesus have put on.
There is neither bond nor free,
male nor female, Lord, in thee.

Love, like death, hath all destroyed,
rendered all distinctions void.
Names and sects and parties fall;
thou, O Christ, art all in all!

—Charles Wesley, *Hymns and Sacred Poems* (1740)

We've a story to tell to the nations,
that shall turn their hearts to the right,

a story of truth and mercy,
a story of peace and light. . . .

We've a song to be sung to the nations,
that shall lift their hearts to the Lord,
a song that shall conquer evil
and shatter the spear and sword.

We've a Savior to show to the nations,
who the path of sorrow has trod,
   that all of the world's great peoples
   might come to the truth of God:
   For the darkness shall turn to dawning,
   and the dawning to noonday bright;
   and Christ's great kingdom shall come on earth,
   the kingdom of love and light.
   H. Ernest Nichol, in *The Sunday School Hymnary*
   (London, 1896)

Charles Wesley and H. Ernest Nichol explore perennial themes: mutual love, the Spirit's gifts, unity and equality in Christ, Christ demolishing dividing walls, and our mission to tell Christ's story, hoping it will turn hearers toward peace and "the right" (not the political "right," but "what is right, not wrong").

A Cautionary Note

Before going farther, a word of caution: Hymns on the church mostly describe what Christian communities are called to be, not necessarily what they are. Self-critical hymns that get into hymnals are mostly about sin—personal or (vaguely) corporate. But today's congregations and denominations are like the church in ancient Corinth: called to be saints and filled with spiritual gifts, but subject to quarrels, divisions, and other kinds of bad behavior (1 Cor. 1:2–7, 11; 5:1, 9–13; 6:7: 11:17–22).

To keep us down to earth, here are some church-critical entries in recent hymnals. Fred Pratt Green invites us (collectively) to ask Christ to increase our awareness tenfold "when the church of Jesus shuts its outer door" because traffic noise is disturbing worship, when devotion "soars high above this hungry, suffering world of ours," or when our offerings of money, time, and talents "serve to salve our conscience, to our secret shame."[1] In another of his hymns, the singers compare themselves to Christians they most admire:

> We marvel how your saints became
> in hindrances more sure;
> whose joyful virtues put to shame
> the casual way we wear your name,
> and by our faults obscure
> your power to cleanse and cure.[2]

Also in the context of public worship, Thomas H. Troeger invites us to pray in personal terms:

> Save me from the soothing sin
> of the empty cultic deed
> and the pious, babbling din
> of the claimed but unlived creed.
> Let my actions, Lord, express
> what my tongue and lips profess.[3]

And one of my hymns affirms that:

> Christ bears the Church, corrupted or conforming,
> obsessed with trifles, blessing greed and war.
> His love outwits us, spinning gold from straw
> through saints and prophets, praying and reforming.[4]

In another hymn:

> We come with self-inflicted pains
> of broken trust and chosen wrong,
> half-free, half-bound by inner chains,
> by social forces swept along,
> by powers and systems close confined,
> yet seeking hope for humankind.

Great God, in Christ you call our name
and then receive us as your own,
not through some merit, right or claim,
but by your gracious love alone.
We strain to glimpse your mercy seat
and find you kneeling at our feet.[5]

Mutual Love

Mutual love entails acceptance, forgiving others, and accepting forgiveness, as in these hymns by Fred Kaan and Rosamond Herklots, and in one of my own hymns about life-partner covenants:

Help us accept each other as Christ accepted us;
teach us as sister, brother each person to embrace.
Be present, God, among us and bring us to believe
we are ourselves accepted and meant to love and live.

Let your acceptance change us, so that we may be moved
in living situations to do the truth in love;
to practice your acceptance until we know by heart
the table of forgiveness and laughter's healing art.[6]

"Forgive our sins as we forgive,"
you taught us, Lord, to pray;
but you alone can grant us grace
to live the words we say.

How can your pardon reach and bless
the unforgiving heart
that broods on wrongs and will not let
old bitterness depart?

In blazing light your cross reveals
the truth we dimly knew:
what trivial debts are owed to us,
how great our debt to you!

Lord, cleanse the depths within our souls
and bid resentment cease.
Then, bound by all the bonds of love,
our lives will spread your peace.[7]

"Forgive Our Sins, as We Forgive," by Rosamond Herklots (1905–87). Reproduced
by permission of Oxford University Press. All rights reserved.

When love is tried
as loved-ones change,
hold still to hope,
though all seems strange,
till ease returns
and love grows wise
through listening ears
and opened eyes.

When love is torn,
and trust betrayed,
pray strength to love
till torments fade,
till lovers keep
no score of wrong,
but hear through pain
love's Easter song.[8]

Mutual love also involves mutual service, as in Richard Gillard's widely published "Servant Song," which recognizes that giving service can be more comfortable than letting someone serve us:

Brother, sister, let me serve you.
Let me be as Christ to you.
Pray that I might have the grace
to let you be my servant too.

We are pilgrims on a journey.
We are friends along the road.
We are here to help each other
walk the mile and bear the load.

I will hold the Christ-light for you
in the night time of your fear.
I will hold my hand out to you,
speak the peace you long to hear.

I will weep when you are weeping.
When you laugh I'll laugh with you.
I will share your joy and sorrow
'till we've seen this journey through.[9]

Mutual love is at the heart of church politics. Practicing it among ourselves prepares us to go beyond ourselves:

Joined in community, treasured and fed,
may we discover gifts in each other,
willing to lead and be led.

Rich in diversity, help us to live
closer than neighbors, open to strangers,
able to clash and forgive.

Glad of tradition, help us to see
in all life's changing, where you are leading,
where our best efforts should be.

Spirit, unite us; make us, by grace,
willing and ready, Christ's living body,
loving the whole human race.[10]

I'll end this chapter by looking at one of Fred Pratt Green's most widely published hymns, "The Church of Christ in Every Age." It begins by depicting the church, not simply in a changing world but "beset by change"—surrounded and relentlessly assailed:

The church of Christ in every age,
beset by change but Spirit-led,
must claim and test its heritage
and keep on rising from the dead.

The phrase "claim *and* test" is worth careful thought, while the final line contains a quiet detonation—*"keep on rising* from the dead" (emphases mine). Resurrection cannot happen before death! In singing these words we are saying what few congregations want to contemplate, that "in every age" churches die.

The second stanza was prompted by a piece of graffiti in what was then a war zone—Belfast, Northern Ireland. It read: "IS THERE LIFE BEFORE DEATH?"

> Across the world, across the street,
> 　the victims of injustice cry
> for shelter and for bread to eat,
> 　and never live until they die.

The Belfast question is pointed and powerful. But moving it from wall to hymn and changing it from question to statement made it unexpectedly problematic. In a conversation about this stanza, someone reminded me that many of the poorest people in the world joyfully testify that in Christ they have found abundant life here and now. By that time, sadly, Fred Pratt Green was no longer writing, so I couldn't discuss the matter with him. He often revised his work in response to comments and had a keen ear for word meanings and social issues. Had he heard the critic, he might well have revised the hymn. Perhaps "and hope to live before they die" would be a suitable revision.

The first version of this hymn had an additional stanza at this point, in language common until the 1970s, which would nowadays need to be revised. Using the metaphor of sin as sickness, it pointed to "deeper ills" than poverty:

> And all men suffer deeper ills:
> 　for there's a fever in our blood
> that prostitutes our human skills
> 　and poisons all our brotherhood.

After this stanza was omitted and the original order revised, Fred Pratt Green came to prefer the now standard version. But the omitted lines give helpful background to the line "can cure the fever in our blood" in the remaining stanzas, below:

> Then let the servant church arise,
>   a caring church that longs to be
> a partner in Christ's sacrifice,
>   and clothed in Christ's humanity.
>
> For Christ alone, whose blood was shed,
>   can cure the fever in our blood,
> and teach us how to share our bread
>   and feed the starving multitude.
>
> We have no mission but to serve
>   in full obedience to our Lord:
> to care for all, without reserve,
>   and spread his liberating word.[11]

To Do and Discuss

1. What could be our own "empty cultic deeds" and "claimed but unlived creeds" (p. 26)? How can empty deeds be filled and unlived creeds be lived?
2. What does it mean to be in Christ, "brothers," "sisters," "pilgrims," "servants," or "friends"? Tease out their meanings. How do they differ? What would be persuasive evidence that we are any of these?
3. Invite people of different ages and viewpoints to explore the meaning of being swept along by social forces and confined by systems and powers (p. 26).
4. How can we discover gifts in each other, be rich in diversity, and live closer than neighbors, open to strangers, able to clash and forgive (p. 29)?
5. "For Christ *alone* . . . can teach us how to share our bread" (see above). Is this true? How?

5

Worship

Jesus, we look to thee,
  thy promised presence claim!
Thou in the midst of us shalt be,
  assembled in thy name.
  Thy name salvation is,
  which here we come to prove;
Thy name is life, and health, and peace,
  and everlasting love.

  Not in the name of pride
  or selfishness we meet.
From nature's paths we turn aside,
  and worldly thoughts forget.
  We meet, the grace to take
  which thou hast freely given.
We meet on earth for thy dear sake,
  that we may meet in heaven.

  Present we know thou art,
  but O thyself reveal!
Now, Lord, let every bounding heart
  the mighty comfort feel.
  O may thy quickening voice
  The death of sin remove,
and bid our inmost souls rejoice
  in hope of perfect love!

—Charles Wesley (1707–88)

In Wesley's hymn we worship, not to escape from life, but in hope of hearing Christ's "quickening voice" and "proving" ("experiencing") Christ's living presence. We turn aside, not from everyday life, but from the worldly ways of unredeemed human nature.

For most Christians, public worship is like breakfast: essential, familiar, frequently unexciting, occasionally enlivened by tasty variations. Like many a piece of furniture, worship comes with a notice saying "Assembly required." In continuity with Wesley ("assembled in thy name"), today's hymns assume an intentional assembly, potentially life changing to all whom God gathers in. Here is a variation on this theme, from Marty Haugen:

> Here in this place, new light is streaming,
>   now is the darkness vanished away.
> See, in this space, our fears and our dreamings,
>   brought here to you in the light of this day.
>   Gather us in—the lost and forsaken,
>   gather us in—the blind and the lame.
>   Call to us now, and we shall awaken,
>   we shall arise at the sound of our name.
>
> Here we will take the wine and the water,
>   here we will take the bread of new birth.
> Here you shall call your sons and your daughters,
>   call us anew to be salt for the earth.
>   Give us to drink the wine of compassion,
>   give us to eat the bread that is you.
>   Nourish us well, and teach us to fashion
>   lives that are holy and hearts that are true.[1]

From England, Fred Pratt Green describes what we hope to find when God gathers us in. He counters nervous, unscriptural requests for God to "be with us" with a ringing affirmation echoing Wesley's "Present we know thou art":

> *God is here!* As we, God's people
>   meet to offer praise and prayer,

may we find in fuller measure
    what it is in Christ we share:
Here, as in the world around us,
    all our varied skills and arts
wait the coming of the Spirit
    into open minds and hearts.

Here are symbols to remind us
    of our lifelong need of grace;
here are table, font and pulpit,
    here the cross has central place.
Here in honesty of preaching,
    here in silence, as in speech,
here in newness and renewal
    God the Spirit comes to each . . .

Here our children find a welcome
    in the Shepherd's flock and fold;
here as bread and wine are taken,
    Christ sustains us as of old.
Here the servants of the Servant
    seek in worship to explore
what it means in daily living
    to believe and to adore.[2]

Worship requires a space in which to assemble, and worshipers are apt to get deeply attached to a purpose-built space, even as they affirm that people matter more than buildings. From Holland, former Jesuit Huub Oosterhuis demystifies every Gothic spire and Protestant pile with the following, which I first came across in a Mennonite hymnal:

What is this place where we are meeting?
Only a house, the earth its floor,
walls and a roof sheltering people,
windows for light, an open door.
Yet it becomes a body that lives
    when we are gathered here,
    and know our God is near.

> And we accept bread at this table,
>> broken and shared, a living sign.
> Here in this world, dying and living,
>> we are each other's bread and wine.
> This is the place where we can receive
>> what we need to increase:
>> our justice and God's peace.[3]

Having gathered, then what? I'll take some of my cues from Fred Pratt Green's "God is here!" (above).

"Here in Silence, as in Speech"

Like dolphins, Christians live in one element and breathe in another. Daily immersed in our culture, we surface in worship, needing the life-giving air of God's reality. We do not want to escape from life but to gain Christ's perspective on it:

> Come and find the quiet center
>> in the crowded life we lead,
> find the room for hope to enter,
>> find the frame where we are freed:
>> clear the chaos and the clutter,
>> clear our eyes, that we can see
>>> all the things that really matter,
>>> be at peace, and simply be.
>
> Silence is a friend who claims us,
>> cools the heat and slows the pace.
> God it is who speaks and names us,
>> knows our being, touches base,
>> making space within our thinking,
>> lifting shades to show the sun,
>>> raising courage when we're shrinking,
>>> finding scope for faith begun.[4]

Song, dance, and prayer can also help us regain Christ's perspective:

As a chalice cast of gold,
   burnished, bright and brimmed with wine,
make me, Lord, as fit to hold
   grace and truth and love divine.
      Let my praise and worship start
      with the cleansing of my heart . . .

When I bend upon my knees,
   clasp my hands or bow my head,
let my spoken, public pleas
   be directly, simply said,
      free of tangled words that mask
      what my soul would plainly ask.

When I dance or chant your praise,
   when I sing a song or hymn,
when I preach your loving ways,
   let my heart add its Amen.
      Let each cherished, outward rite
      thus reflect your inward light.[5]

"In Honesty of Preaching . . . the Cross Has Central Place"

From Judaism, Christian worship inherits the public speaking of
Scripture (Jewish and Christian) and Scripture-focused speech variously called preaching, exposition, and proclamation. Many hymns
imply or contain proclamation, even when cast as prayer or praise:

Still your children wander homeless;
   still the hungry cry for bread;
   still the captives long for freedom;
still in grief we mourn our dead.
As you, Lord, in deep compassion
   healed the sick and freed the soul,
   use the love your Spirit kindles,
saving, healing, making whole.

As we worship, grant us vision,
   till your love's revealing light,

in its height and depth and greatness
dawns upon our wakened sight;
making known the needs and burdens
    your compassion bids us bear,
    stirring us to joyful striving
your abundant life to share.[6]

In Christian preaching, the cross of Christ is central. In seven four-line stanzas, Thomas Troeger invites us to praise:

The gracious power that tumbles walls of fear . . .
    Persistent truth that opens fisted minds . . .
        Inclusive love, . . . oblivious to gender, wealth, . . . or place . . .
        The word of faith that claims us as God's own . . .
    The tide of grace that laps at every shore . . .
All of the above and their source . . . Christ, the crucified . . .

In the final stanza we praise the living Christ and announce the gospel to the world. Each stanza ends with the emphatic refrain:
    We praise you, Christ! Your cross has made us one![7] (Full text, chapter 8)

"Symbols to Remind Us"—Font

I taught for seven years in a Presbyterian theological seminary. The chapel font stands either just inside the door or by the Communion table or pulpit at the other end. On top of its three-foot-high stand sits a large transparent bowl of water. The chapel font is not for baptism, which in Presbyterian churches is administered in a local congregation. It is, instead, a tangible reminder of Christ's summons to discipleship and our response as we enter (join) the church through baptism or claim its promises for our children. When the font stands inside the door, worshipers often dip their fingers in the water as they enter or leave. When it stands by the table or pulpit, worship leaders sometimes hand-splash water as they declare God's forgiveness or shout, "Remember your baptism!" From the United States, Ronald S. Cole-Turner has us sing the church's loving song to a baptized child.

From Scotland and Spain, John Bell, Graham Moule, and Cesáreo Gabaráin echo Christ's call to all of us:

> Child of blessing, child of promise,
>   baptized with the Spirit's sign;
> with this water God has sealed you
>   unto love and grace divine . . .
>
> Child of joy, our dearest treasure,
>   God's you are, from God you came.
> Back to God we humbly give you;
>   live as one who bears Christ's name.
>
> Child of God your loving Parent,
>   learn to know whose child you are.
> Grow to laugh and sing and worship,
>   trust and love God more than all.[8]

Will you come and follow me if I but call your name?
Will you go where you don't know and never be the same?
Will you let my love be shown? Will you let my name be known?
Will you let my life be grown in you and you in me?
Will you leave yourself behind if I but call your name?
Will you care for cruel and kind and never be the same?
Will you risk the hostile stare should your life attract or scare?
Will you let me answer prayer in you and you in me?[9] (Full text, chapter 8)

> Lord, when you came to the seashore,
> you weren't seeking the wise or the wealthy,
> but only asking that I might follow.
>
> Lord, you knew what my boat carried:
> neither money nor weapons for fighting,
> but nets for fishing, my daily labor.
> **O Lord, in my eyes you were gazing.**
> **Kindly smiling, my name you were saying.**
> **All I treasured, I have left on the sand there.**
> **Close to you, I will find other seas.**[10]

"Lifelong Need of Grace"—Table

A distinguishing mark of almost all Christian worship is a symbolic meal of bread and wine variously known as the Lord's Supper, Holy Communion, or Eucharist. It is one of the earliest recorded Christian practices (1 Cor. 11), traced by the apostle Paul back to Jesus himself (vv. 23–25):

> An upper room did our Lord prepare
> for those he loved until the end:
> and his disciples still gather there,
> to celebrate their risen Friend. . . .
>
> And after supper he washed their feet,
> for service, too, is sacrament.
> In him our joy shall be made complete
> sent out to serve, as he was sent.[11]

Often the meal gets too symbolic: *bread* becomes tiny precut cubes, wafers dissolved on the tongue, or the smallest morsel that can be broken off without crumbling onto the floor; *wine* becomes the smallest possible sip or a droplet in a tiny prepoured glass. Fred Kaan offers an exuberant antidote to such petty scrupulosity:

> Let us talents and tongues employ,
> reaching out with a shout of joy:
> bread is broken, the wine is poured,
> Christ is spoken and seen and heard. . . .
>
> Jesus calls us in, sends us out
> bearing fruit in a world of doubt,
> gives us love to tell, bread to share:
> God (Immanuel) everywhere!
> **Jesus lives again; earth can breathe again.**
> **Pass the Word around:** *loaves abound!*[12]

In contrast to some of their predecessors, today's Communion hymns are more aware that "communion" implies "community." My own hymn "I Come with Joy," begins with "I" and progresses to end with "we":

I come with joy, a child of God . . .
The love that made us, makes us one . . .
Together met, together bound . . .
we'll go with joy[13]
(Full text, chapter 8)

From the Roman Catholic liturgical renewal movement, Omer
Westendorf and John Foley also emphasize how Communion declares
and enacts our unity in Christ:

You satisfy the hungry heart with gift of finest wheat.
Come give to us, O saving Lord, the bread of life to eat.
Is not the cup we bless and share
the blood of Christ outpoured?
Do not one cup, one loaf declare
our oneness in one Lord?

You give yourself to us, O Lord,
then selfless let us be,
to serve each other in your name
in truth and charity.
You satisfy the hungry heart with gift of finest wheat,
Come give to us O saving Lord, the bread of life to eat.[14]

One bread, one body, one Lord of all,
one cup of blessing, which we bless.
And we, though many, throughout the earth,
we are one body in this one Lord.
Gentile or Jew, servant or free, woman or man, no more.
Many the gifts, many the works, one in the Lord of all.
Grain for the fields, scattered and grown, gathered to one, for all.
One bread, one body, one Lord of all,
one cup of blessing, which we bless.
And we, though many, throughout the earth,
we are one body in this one Lord.[15]

With striking originality, Jaroslav Vajda offers a Communion
hymn that can be understood in both individual and corporate senses.
Titled "Now," it is a series of phrases without a single verb:

Now . . . the silence . . . the peace . . . the empty hands uplifted
. . . the kneeling . . . the plea . . . the Father's arms in welcome

. . . the hearing . . . the power . . . the vessel brimmed for pouring . . . the body . . . the blood . . . the joyful celebration . . . the
wedding . . . the songs . . . the heart forgiven leaping . . . the
Spirit's visitation . . . the Son's epiphany . . . the Father's blessing . . . Now . . . Now . . . Now . . .

(For the full text, with Vajda's companion hymn, "Then," see chapter 8.)[16]

A final Communion hymn that must be mentioned is Tom Colvin's
"Jesu, Jesu" (pronounced "Yay-*soo*"). It understands John's account
of the footwashing (John 13:1–17) as the model for Christian service
within and beyond the church. As such, it repays careful attention, as
for example in the phrases "*silently* washes," "washing their feet,"
"puts us on our knees," "nearby and far away," and, more controver-
sial, perhaps, "as though we are slaves" [emphasis mine]:

Jesu, Jesu, fill us with your love,
show us how to serve
the neighbors we have from you.

Kneels at the feet of his friends,
silently washes their feet,
master who acts as a slave to them.

Neighbors are wealthy and poor,
varied in color and race,
neighbors are nearby and far away.

These are the ones we will serve,
these are the ones we will love;
all these are neighbors to us and you.

Loving puts us on our knees,
serving as though we are slaves;
this is the way we will live with you.

Kneel at the feet of our friends,
silently washing their feet;
this is the way we will live with you.

**Jesu, Jesu, fill us with your love,
show us how to serve
the neighbors we have from you.**[17]

Copyright © 1969 by Hope Publishing Company, Carol Stream, IL 60188. All rights reserved. Used by permission.

Table Prayer

At Christ's Supper, the best dinner-table conversation is prayer. We pray for one another, including members and friends who are suffering:

> O Christ, the healer, we have come
>   to pray for health, to plead for friends.
> How can we fail to be restored,
>   when reached by love that never ends?
>
> From every ailment flesh endures
>   our bodies clamor to be freed;
> yet in our hearts we would confess
>   that wholeness is our deepest need.
>
> How strong, O Lord, are our desires,
>   how weak our knowledge of ourselves!
> Release in us those healing truths
>   unconscious pride resists or shelves.
>
> Grant that we all, made one in faith,
>   in your community may find
> the wholeness that, enriching us,
>   shall reach the whole of humankind.[18]

As I write this book, a beloved friend and spouse are bearing the outrageous damage caused by Alzheimer's disease, while a close relative struggles with sight and mobility impairment and distressing lapses of memory. In the pain and exhaustion of suffering and caregiving, all words fail. When time allows space for song, Mary Louise Bringle offers a timely hymn:

> When memory fades and recognition falters,
>   when eyes we love grow dim, and minds, confused . . .

O God of life and healing peace, empower us
    with patient courage, by your grace infused.

As frailness grows, and youthful strengths diminish
    in weary arms, which worked their earnest fill . . .
We grieve their waning . . .

but determine to affirm that—

Within your Spirit, goodness lives unfading.
    The past and future mingle into one.
All joys remain, unshadowed light pervading.
    No valued deed will ever be undone. . . .[19]

Prayer also reaches far beyond the assembled company because, in Tom Colvin's words, "neighbors are nearby and far away" (above, p. 41). Every time I worship in a congregation I ask, "Where will worship take us today?" Will we range in imagination beyond those assembled here, beyond our walls, our localities, our hurt and suffering? Will prayer demonstrate that we love our enemies? Will it take us beyond patriotism and civil religion? Will we thank God for, and pray or, other Christians, other faiths, other cultures and countries— whether they do or don't flit into our twenty-four-hour news-cycle headlines? From the Iona Community Wild Goose Resource Group, John Bell and Graham Maule call us to impassioned prayer:

Feel for the people we most avoid—
    Strange or bereaved or never employed.
Feel for the women and feel for the men
    who fear that their living is all in vain . . .

Feel for the parents who lost their child,
    feel for the woman whom men have defiled.
Feel for the baby for whom there's no breast,
    and feel for the weary who find no rest . . .

Feel for the lives by life confused.
    Riddled with doubt, in loving abused;
Feel for the lonely heart, conscious of sin,
    which longs to be pure but fears to begin . . .

Christ's is the world in which we move.
Christ's are the folk we're summoned to love,
Christ's is the voice which calls us to care,
and Christ is the One who meets us here.
  To the lost Christ shows his face;
    to the unloved he gives his embrace;
  to those who cry in pain or disgrace,
    Christ, makes, with His friends, a touching place.[20]

"What It Means in Daily Living"

When worship fulfills its purpose, a crowd that assembles becomes
a body that leaves. In Albert Bayly's words, it is "called from worship unto service . . . love in living deeds to show (see p. 93)"[21] As
Fred Kaan has already reminded us, Jesus calls us in and sends us
out, "bearing fruit in a world of doubt." (p. 39). As we go, his words
prepare us to engage in God's mission:

Now let us from this table rise
  renewed in body, mind, and soul;
with Christ we die and live again,
  his selfless love has made us whole.

With minds alert, upheld by grace,
  to spread the Word in speech and deed,
we follow in the steps of Christ,
  at one with all in hope and need.

To fill each human house with love,
  it is the sacrament of care;
the work that Christ began to do
  we humbly pledge ourselves to share.

Then grant us grace, Companion-God,
  to choose again the pilgrim way
and help us to accept with joy
  the challenge of tomorrow's day.[22]

Copyright © 1968 by Hope Publishing Company for the U.S.A. and Canada and by
Stainer & Bell for all other territories. All rights reserved. Used by permission.

To Do and Discuss

1. "Public worship is like breakfast: essential, familiar, frequently unexciting, occasionally enlivened by tasty variations." Yes? No? So what?
2. Read aloud and then discuss "God is here" (pp. 33–34) and "What is this place?" (p. 34).
3. Share a hymn quoted in this chapter that moves, teaches, annoys, or encourages you. Why?
4. What fruit can Christians bear in a world of doubt (p. 39)?
5. What can we do to demonstrate that loaves abound (p. 39)?
6. Ponder the meaning of "Daily immersed in our culture, we surface in worship needing the life-giving air of God's reality" (p. 35).
7. Visit another congregation and ask people to visit yours, pondering how far—and how—each congregation gives the impression of not wanting to escape from life but gain Christ's perspective on it (p. 35).
8. Ask "Where will worship take us today?—and how (p. 43)?"

6

Witness

O Spirit of the living God,
in all the fullness of thy grace,
wherever human feet have trod,
descend on our apostate race.

Give tongues of fire and hearts of love,
to preach the reconciling word;
give power and unction[1] from above,
whene'er the joyful sound is heard.

Be darkness, at thy coming, light;
confusion, order in thy path;
souls without strength inspire with might,
bid mercy triumph over wrath.

Baptize the nations; far and nigh
the triumphs of the cross record;
the Name of Jesus glorify,
till every kindred call him Lord.

God from eternity hath willed
all flesh shall his salvation see;
so be the Father's love fulfilled,
the Savior's sufferings crowned through thee.

—James Montgomery (1771–1854)

*M*ontgomery's hymn echoes two directives from the risen
Christ: "Go therefore and make disciples of all nations, baptiz-

ing them in the name of the Father and of the Son and of the Holy
Spirit" (Matt. 28:19), and "You will receive power when the Holy
Spirit has come upon you; and you will be my witnesses in Jerusalem,
in all Judea and Samaria, and to the ends of the earth" (Acts 1:8).

Drawing on the Pentecost story (Acts 2), Montgomery affirms
that only the Spirit can empower us to be Christ's witnesses. Only
the Spirit can bring rebirth to human beings who have turned away
(become apostate) from God. Only the Spirit can "give tongues of fire
and hearts of love, to preach the reconciling word." Only the Spirit
can change weakness into strength, rage into mercy, confusion into
order, and darkness into light.

Some recent hymns reecho these themes. Matthew 28:19, often
called the Great Commission, is the foundation of Jeffery Rowthorn's
"Lord, You Give the Great Commission," where every stanza answers
a statement with a prayer and ends by asking: "With the Spirit's gifts
empower us for the work of ministry":

> Lord, you give the great commission:
>   "Heal the sick and preach the word!"—
> help us witness to your purpose
>   with renewed integrity . . .

> Lord, you make the common holy:
>   "This my body, this my blood."
> Let us all, for earth's true glory,
>   daily lift life heavenward,
> asking that the world around us
>   share your children's liberty . . .

> Lord, you show us love's true measure:
>   "Father, what they do, forgive."
> Yet we hoard as private treasure
>   all that you so freely give.
> May your care and mercy lead us
>   to a just society.
>   **With the Spirit's gifts empower us**
>   **for the work of ministry.**[2]

Drawing on Paul's description of the one Spirit giving many gifts
(1 Cor. 12:4–11), Rusty Edwards declares that the Great Commission
obliges us to work together:

> We all are called to service,
>   to witness in God's name.
> Our ministries are different.
>   Our purpose is the same:
> to touch the lives of others
>   with God's surprising grace . . .

Because—

> We all are one in mission.
>   We all are one in call,
> our varied gifts united
>   by Christ the Lord of all.[3]

An Advent hymn by Ruth Duck points to another "great commission," Jesus' synagogue sermon and its source (Luke 4:14–21; Isa.
61:1–4), linked with the call, "Arise, shine; for your light has come"
(Isa. 60:1):

> Arise, your light has come!
>   Fling wide the prison door;
> proclaim the captive's liberty,
>   good tidings to the poor.

> Arise, your light has come!
>   All you in sorrow born,
> bind up the brokenhearted ones
>   and comfort those who mourn.[4]

Ruth Duck's word choices echo Isaiah 61:1–4 (liberty, captives,
brokenhearted, comfort all who mourn). They also reflect the context in which today's Christians bear witness to Jesus, which includes
war, hunger, terror, genocide, and oppression. William Watkins Reid
Jr. explores such themes in a hymn whose opening lines specifically
reject flag-waving nationalism (emphasis mine):

O God of *every* nation,
   of *every* race and land,
redeem the whole creation
   with your almighty hand;
where hate and fear divide us
   and bitter threats are hurled,
in love and mercy guide us
   and heal our strife-torn world.

From search for wealth and power
   and scorn of truth and right,
from trust in bombs that shower
   destruction through the night,
from pride of race and nation
   and blindness to your way,
deliver *every* nation,
   eternal God, we pray!

In the era of mounted cavalry, officers sometimes rattled their sabers in their scabbards as a threat to use military force. Reid's hymn continues with this metaphor:

Lord, strengthen all who labor
   that we may find release
from fear of rattling saber,
   from dread of war's increase . . .
Keep bright in us the vision
   of days when war shall cease,
when hatred and division
   give way to love and peace.[5]

Peace with Justice

Though "O God of Every Nation" is a hymn for today, it dates from 1958, in language reflecting 1940s warfare. Perhaps the next generation of hymnals will enable us to lament and pray about genocide, rape as a weapon of war, terror as technique, coerced population flight (hypocritically called "ethnic cleansing"), and so-called "smart" bombardment, whose frequent noncombatant deaths are shrugged off as "collateral damage." In the hymn renaissance Christian witness consistently sings a longing for peace, not merely as the cessation of conflict, but linked with sharing and social fairness, as in the following, from Ruth Duck, Miriam Therese Winter, and Fred Kaan:

> When bodies shiver in the night
>   and weary wait for morning,
> when children have no bread but tears,
>   and war-horns sound their warning,
> God calls humanity to wake,
>   to join in common labor,
> that all may have abundant life,
>   in oneness with their neighbor.
>
> God calls humanity to join
>   as partners in creating
> a future free from want or fear,
>   life's goodness celebrating.
> That new world beckons from afar,
>   invites our shared endeavor
> that all might have abundant life
>   and peace endure forever.[6]

> O for a world where goods are shared
>   and misery relieved,
> where truth is spoken, children spared,
>   equality achieved.
>
> O for a world preparing for
>   God's glorious reign of peace,
> where time and tears will be no more—
>   and all but love will cease.[7]

> For the healing of the nations,
>   God, we pray with one accord,
> for a just and equal sharing
>   of the things that earth affords.
> To a life of love in action
>   help us rise and pledge our word.

Lead us forward into freedom,
    from despair your world release,
that, redeemed from war and hatred,
    all may come and go in peace.
Show us how through care and goodness
    fear will die and hope increase.

All that kills abundant living,
    let it from the earth be banned:
pride of status, race or schooling,
    dogmas that obscure your plan.
In our common quest for justice
    may we hallow brief life's span.[8]

In another hymn, Fred Kaan gives us vivid imagery and careful word choices to sing about the blessings and ambiguities of harvest. We begin by uniting in praise to God, our Creator, as we

. . . stand to recall with thanksgiving
that to God all seasons belong.

In the second stanza we give thanks for "the joy and abundance of crops," foodstuffs in well-stocked shops, and "food that is stored in our larders" (cool-storage cupboards, increasingly replaced by refrigerators). If we expect to continue singing in that vein, we are in for a surprise—

But also of need and starvation
    we sing with concern and despair,
of skills that are used for destruction,
    of land that is burnt and laid bare.

Note the prophetic awareness of the abuse of economic power in what follows:

We cry for the plight of the hungry
    while harvests are *left on the field,*
for orchards neglected and wasting,
    for produce *from markets withheld.*

We are now ready for a global vision, as the word "thanksgiving" reappears in one of the finest couplets of twentieth-century hymnody:

> The song grows in depth and in wideness;
>   the earth and its people are one.
> There can be no *thanks* without *giving,*
>   *no words without deeds that are done.*[9]
>   (Full text, chapter 8)

Fred Kaan's allusion to "pride of . . . race" (above, p. 51) is a reminder that institutional and attitudinal racism are major components of injustice. Shirley Murray offers a thought-provoking meditation. She begins by seeing gender and skin color as precious aspects of God's image, in which all human beings are created:

> O God, we bear the imprint of your face:
>   the colors of our skin are your design,
> and what we have of beauty in our race
>   as man or woman, you alone define,
>   who stretched a living fabric on our frame
>   and gave to each a language and a name.

When racism divides us, ethnic diversity is not celebrated, but feared. And when racism is backed by state-sponsored inequality, people are victimized for claiming their God-given identity, their own name:

> Where we are torn and pulled apart by hate
>   because our race, our skin is not the same;
> while we are judged unequal by the state
>   and victims made because we own our name,
>   humanity reduced to little worth,
>   dishonored is your living face on earth.

In the final stanza, our yardstick for what it means to be human is Jesus' way of living (his humanity), not his male gender. As in Mark 3:33–35, our true family is not a biological relationship but the household of faith. And failure to learn how to love will have mortal consequences:

O God, we share the image of your Son
   whose flesh and blood are ours, whatever skin;
in his humanity we find our own,
    and in his family our proper kin:
      Christ is the brother we still crucify,
      his love the language we must learn *or die*.[10]

Scotland's Iona Community is Jesus-focused and Christ-centered.
A hymn by John Bell and Graham Maule puts us *alongside* the risen
Christ, in the streets of our cities and towns:

Jesus Christ is waiting, waiting in the streets;
   No one is his neighbor, all alone he eats.
    Listen, Lord Jesus, I am lonely too.
    Make me, friend or stranger,
      fit to wait on you.

Jesus Christ is raging, raging in the streets,
   Where injustice spirals, and real hope retreats.
    Listen, Lord Jesus, I am angry too.
    In the kingdom's causes
      let me rage with you. . . .

Jesus Christ is dancing, dancing in the streets,
   Where each sign of hatred he, with love, defeats.
    Listen, Lord Jesus, I should triumph too.
    On suspicion's graveyard
      let me dance with you.[11]

God's peace (*shalom*) includes social justice. Here is a black American slave song placed in dialogue with Albert Bayly's interpretation
of Micah 6:6–8:

What does the Lord require
for praise and offering?
What sacrifice, desire
or tribute bid you bring?

Do justly!
Love mercy!
Walk humbly with your God!

When Israel was in Egypt's land,
(Let my people go!)
oppressed so hard they could not stand,
(Let my people go!)
   Go down, Moses,
      way down in Egypt's land;
      tell old Pharaoh
   to let my people go!

Rulers of earth, give ear!
Should you not justice know?
Will God your pleading hear,
while crime and cruelty grow?

No more shall they in bondage toil,
(Let my people go!)
let them come out with Egypt's spoil,
(Let my people go!)

Leaders in wealth and trade,
for whom the workers toil,
think not to win God's aid
if lies your commerce soil:

As Israel stood by the water's side,
(Let my people go!)
at God's command it did divide,
(Let my people go!)

Still down the ages ring
the prophet's stern commands:
to merchant, worker, king,
he brings God's high demands.

When they had reached the other shore,
(Let my people go!)

they sang a song of triumph o'er,
(Let my people go!)
Go down, Moses,
    way down in Egypt's land;
    tell old Pharaoh
to let my people go!

How shall our life fulfill
God's law so hard and high?
Let Christ endue our will
with grace to fortify:
Then justly,
    in mercy,
        we'll humbly walk with God.[12]

Years ago, when I went door-to-door in urban Britain collecting for Christian Aid (a U.K. ecumenical agency), I found that people with low or fixed incomes gave more, proportionately, than people living in relative comfort. A hymn by José Antonio Olivar gives a timely reminder that people living in poverty can be subjects of sharing, not objects of charity:

When the poor ones who have nothing still are giving;
when the thirsty pass the cup, water to share;
when the wounded offer others strength and healing:
    we see God, here by our side, walking our way.

When compassion gives the suffering consolation;
when expecting brings to birth hope that was lost;
when we choose love, not the hatred all around us:
    we see God, here by our side, walking our way.

When our spirits, like a chalice, brim with gladness;
when our voices, full and clear, sing out the truth;
when our longings, free from envy, seek the humble:
    we see God, here by our side, walking our way.[13]

To conclude this section I'll spotlight two perspectives on peace. In one of his finest hymns, the author of "For the Healing of the

Nations" (Fred Kaan) brings peacemaking from an international to an interpersonal level (full text, chapter 8). Using a classic structure for a thematic hymn, the first three stanzas open with the same line, "Put peace into each other's hands"—

> And like a treasure hold it . . .
> With loving expectation . . .
> Like bread we break for sharing . . .

The fourth stanza varies the theme with reference to Holy Communion—

> As at communion, shape your hands
>   into a waiting cradle;
> the gift of Christ receive, revere,
>   united round the table.

The final stanza returns to a variation of the opening line—

> Put Christ into each other's hands;
>   he is love's deepest measure.
> In love make peace, give peace a chance,
>   and share it like a treasure.

In keeping with its theme, the hymn joins nurturing vocabulary with vivid imagery (emphasis mine):

Protect it like a candle flame, with *tenderness* enfold it . . . *like bread we break for sharing*; look people *warmly* in the eye . . . our life is meant for *caring* . . . shape your hands *into a waiting cradle*.

The hymn begins with the supreme value of peace between one person and another (emphasis mine):

> Put peace into each other's hands
> And like a *treasure* hold it—

and ends likewise:

in love make peace, give peace a chance,
and share it like a *treasure*.[14]

With "give peace a chance," Fred Kaan uses his gift of seeing a
deeper meaning in a common phrase—in this case a John Lennon song
title. "Give peace a chance" is the opening line of a song composed
during John Lennon and Yoko Ono's 1969 bed-in protest for peace.
It became for a while an antinuclear campaign slogan, then became
exhausted by repetition. By placing it at the climax of the hymn—and
at the naturally emphatic end of a line—Kaan recredentials its serious
simplicity, whether or not singers know its origin.

England has a hymn that is almost a second national anthem. It
is a poem by William Blake set to C. Hubert H. Parry's stirring tune
JERUSALEM. It begins, "And did those feet in ancient time walk upon
England's mountains green/And was the holy Lamb of God on England's pleasant pastures seen?" During the preparation of the U.S.
Episcopal Church's *Hymnal 1982*, Carl Daw was asked to write a
peace-focus hymn for Parry's tune. Drawing on Isaiah 11:6–7, his
response has been widely published and sung:

O day of peace that dimly shines
    through all our hopes and prayers and dreams,
guide us to justice, truth, and love,
    delivered from our selfish schemes.
May swords of hate fall from our hands,
    our hearts from envy find release,
till by God's grace our warring world
    shall see Christ's promised reign of peace.

Then shall the wolf dwell with the lamb,
    nor shall the fierce devour the small;
as beasts and cattle calmly graze,
    a little child shall lead them all.
Then enemies shall learn to love,
    all creatures find their true accord;
the hope of peace shall be fulfilled,
    for all the earth shall know the Lord.[15]

Copyright © 1982 by Hope Publishing Company, Carol Stream, IL 60188. All rights
reserved. Used by permission.

Discovery, Ambiguity, and Fragility

God, who stretched the spangled heavens,
    infinite in time and place,
flung the suns in burning radiance
    through the silent fields of space:
we, your children in your likeness,
    share inventive powers with you.
Great Creator, still creating,
    show us what we yet may do . . .

We have ventured worlds undreamed of
    since the childhood of our race,
known the ecstasy of winging
    through untraveled realms of space,
probed the secrets of the atom,
    yielding unimagined power,
facing us with life's destruction
    or our most triumphant hour.[16]

Catherine Cameron's phrase "our most triumphant hour" is open to question, but the problems of nuclear power were less evident when she wrote it (1967) than they are now. Cameron's hymn is one of the earliest to recognize that Christian witness takes place amid accelerating discoveries about the universe, combined with the power of human action to damage or destroy our planet. In this, she follows a prescient hymn by Albert Bayly, written in 1945, at the end of the Second World War:

O Lord of every shining constellation
    that wheels in splendor through the midnight sky,
grant us your Spirit's true illumination
    to read the secrets of your work on high.

You, Lord, have made the atom's hidden forces.
    Your laws its mighty energies fulfill;
teach us, to whom you give such rich resources,
    in all we use, to serve your holy will.[17]

Shirley Murray gives us a profound and well-crafted hymn about the need to care for planet Earth. I shall print it in full, then look at it more closely:

> Touch the earth lightly,
> use the earth gently,
> nourish the life of the world in our care:
> gift of great wonder,
> ours to surrender,
> trust for the children tomorrow will bear.
>
> We who endanger,
> who create hunger,
> agents of death for all creatures that live,
> we who would foster
> clouds of disaster,
> God of our planet, forestall and forgive!
>
> Let there be greening,
> birth from the burning,
> water that blesses and air that is sweet,
> health in God's garden,
> hope in God's children,
> regeneration that peace will complete.
>
> God of all living,
> God of all loving,
> God of the seedling, the snow, and the sun,
> teach us, deflect us,
> Christ, reconnect us,
> using us gently, and making us one.[18]

Copyright © 1982 by Hope Publishing Company, Carol Stream, IL 60188. All rights reserved. Used by permission.

The hymn's opening line is an Australian aboriginal saying. As with any good hymn, it claims attention, states the theme, and sets the tone for what follows. Each stanza has two sets of two five-syllable lines followed by a line of ten syllables. Speak the stanzas aloud and you'll hear how their meaning and speech rhythms support each other. The rhythmic pattern is mostly dactylic, a word derived from the Greek word for finger (*dactyl*), because a finger has a long bone followed by two shorter bones, which the speech rhythm (DAH-duh-duh) echoes sonically. In each stanza the first two five-syllable lines are a dactyl followed by a trochee (DAH-duh-duh DAH-duh), giving a feeling of something said but incomplete. The third, ten-syllable line brings completion by uncurling in three dactyls stopped by a final syllable: DAH-duh-duh DAH-duh-duh DAH-duh-duh DAH.

The "light" unstressed endings of the five syllable lines[19] give gentle sounds with gentle meanings (lightly, gently, wonder). In mid-stanza comes an apparent paradox: the "gift of great wonder" is "ours"—not, however, to keep, but to *surrender*, a word suggesting that we let go of it, as much reluctantly as willingly, only for the sake of our children.

The first stanza begins with imperatives: Touch! Use gently! Nourish! The second confesses the human race's failure as planetary guardians, leading with first person plurals whose place in the line gives them natural emphasis: *we who—who—we who*. At the line endings, where full rhymes (moon/June) might sound too pretty for the subject matter, Murray's half rhymes catch attention: *endanger/hunger, foster/disaster*. Depicting human beings as agents of death is sobering but undeniable. In this stanza the first two lines use their rhythms more insistently, as the dactyls (fingers) are pointed in accusation. The fourth and fifth lines vary the pattern by becoming, in effect and rhythm, an extra ten-syllable line, building a long petition that climaxes in the final line with the alliterative, and dramatic, "forestall and forgive!"

The closing stanzas are earnest prayer, mostly reverting to the light, gentle line endings of the first (greening, garden, children, living, loving), backed by other gentle and nurturing word choices (blesses, sweet, health, hope, seedling, snow, sun).

The opening stanzas invite us to play with the related meanings of *trust, agents,* and *foster,* such as parenting, legal guardianship, financial management, and stewardship. In stanza three the word "birth" has overtones of Christian "new birth" language (John 1:12–13 and 3:3–7, 1 Pet. 1:3), followed and paralleled by "regeneration," a technical term whose five-syllable length also suggests that the process takes time.

In the second and final stanzas God in Christ opposes our destructive mismanagement, not violently, but as a skilled judo instructor, who "forestalls" and "deflects" us. And the phrase "use . . . gently" links the opening and closing stanzas. We are called to use the earth gently, so that we can trust Jesus to use us gently and make us one.

Whom Shall I Send?

New hymnody of Christian witness ranges from the Great Commission to urgent calls for deliverance from war, hunger, and oppression; from thanks that include giving to love that overcomes racism; and from peace both interpersonal and international to the care and protection of planet Earth. Returning now to the daily witness of Christian disciples, Caryl Micklem prays with vigorous simplicity. As we take our place as actors in the divine drama, we "play [our] part," not as entertainment, but wholeheartedly, and live out, "act on," our love-script:

> Give to me, Lord, a thankful heart
>   and a discerning mind;
> give, as I play the Christian's part,
> the strength to finish what I start
>   and act on what I find.
>
> When, in the rush of days, my will
>   is habit bound and slow,
> help me to keep in vision still
> what love and power and peace can fill
>   a life that trusts in you.
>
> By your divine and urgent claim,
>   and by your human face,
> kindle our sinking hearts to flame,
> and as you teach the world your name
>   let it become your place.
>
> Jesus, with all your Church I long
>   to see your kingdom come:
> show me your way of righting wrong

and turning sorrow into song
until you bring me home.[20]

Copyright © 1975 by Ruth Micklem. All rights reserved. Used by permission.

This final stanza (of a four-stanza hymn) invites us to ponder together: How, and how far, do we *long* for God's reign to come on earth? What is Jesus' way of righting wrong, and how does it differ from our culture's way? Does turning sorrow into song mean that we overcome it, or beautify the bearing of it?

I was baptized on confession of faith because Jesus had become the central figure in my life, and Christian faith offered a vision and perspective on human existence that convincingly interpreted life's meaning. But when I asked myself what difference Christian faith made to my behavior, the answer—to be honest—was not very much. Centuries of Christianization had brought my church and society to a situation where being a Christian did not appear to be markedly different from being a good person, or even—perish the thought—a nice person! Fred Pratt Green may be responding to this situation when he hears great Christian witnesses showing up our bland use of the word "Christian":

How clear is our vocation, Lord,
when once we heed your call:
to live according to your word,
and daily learn, refreshed, restored,
that you are Lord of all,
and will not let us fall. . . .

We marvel how your saints became
in hindrances more sure;
whose joyful virtues put to shame
the casual way we wear your name,
and by our faults obscure
your power to cleanse and cure.

In what you give us, Lord, to do,
together or alone,
in old routines or ventures new,

> may we not cease to look to you,
> the cross you hung upon—
> all you endeavored, done.[21]

Finally, Daniel Schutte draws on Scripture sources including 1 Samuel 3:1–10 and Isaiah 6:1–8, weaving into hymn-poetry the divine call to go out and serve God's people. The disciple's response moves from statement ("Here I am") to question ("Is it I?") to conditional statement ("I will go . . . if you lead me") in a way that encourages sincerity without grandiosity:

> I, the Lord of snow and rain,
> I have borne my people's pain;
> I have wept for love of them.
>   They turn away.
>
> I will break their hearts of stone,
> give their hearts for love alone.
> I will speak my word to them.
>   Whom shall I send?
>
> **Here I am, Lord. Is it I, Lord?**
> **I have heard you calling in the night.**
> **I will go, Lord, if you lead me.**
> **I will hold your people in my heart.**[22]
>   (Full text, chapter 8)

To Do and Discuss

1. Is nationalism (p. 48) a religion? Has it always been? In other countries? In our own? Invite pro and con thoughts on this or stage a formal or informal debate, with or without a vote.
2. "In the hymn renaissance Christian witness consistently sings a longing for peace, not merely as the cessation of conflict, but linked with sharing and social fairness" (p. 50). How can worship and outreach express such longings?
3. In a group, invite people to meditate on and offer short (twenty-word) "text message" type comments or prayers on "There

can be no thanks without giving" (p. 52) and "Jesus Christ is waiting . . . raging . . . dancing in the streets" (p. 53). The word limit is not a hard rule but meant to encourage brevity and maximum participation.

4. What is the point of singing about peace and justice in a world and culture where churches have little power to bring them about? Work out some "text message" answers to share in public worship.

5. Find and share news stories that connect with the hymns quoted in this chapter.

6. How do Caryl Micklem and Fred Pratt Green (pp. 61–62) assist, deepen, or challenge our daily discipleship?

7. Try acting out "Put peace into each other's hands" (pp. 56–57 and 101).

Praise

The God of Abraham praise,
* who reigns enthroned above;*
Ancient of everlasting days,
*   and God of love;*
Jehovah, great I AM,
* by earth and heaven confessed:*
I bow and bless the sacred Name
*   for ever blessed.*

The God of Abraham praise,
* at whose supreme command*
from earth I rise, and seek the joys
*   at his right hand;*
I all on earth forsake,
* its wisdom, fame and power;*
and him our only portion make,
*   my Shield and Tower.*

Though nature's strength decay,
* and earth and hell withstand,*
to Canaan's bounds I urge my way,
*   at His command.*
The watery deep I pass,
* with Jesus in my view;*
and through the howling wilderness
*   my way pursue.*

The heavenly land I see,
* with peace and plenty blessed:*

a land of sacred liberty
  and endless rest;
there milk and honey flow,
and oil and wine abound,
and trees of life for ever grow,
  with mercy crowned.

There dwells the Lord, our King,
  the Lord, our Righteousness,
triumphant o'er the world and sin,
  the Prince of Peace;
on Zion's sacred height
  his kingdom he maintains,
and, glorious with his saints in light,
  for ever reigns.

Before the Savior's face
  the ransomed nations bow,
o'erwhelmed at his almighty grace,
  for ever new.
He shows his prints of love:
  they kindle to a flame,
and sound through all the worlds above
  the slaughtered Lamb.

The whole triumphant host
  give thanks to God on high;
"Hail, Father, Son, and Holy Ghost"
  they ever cry;
hail, Abraham's God and mine—
  I join the heavenly lays;
all might and majesty are thine,
  and endless praise.

—Thomas Olivers (1725–99)

This is one among several versions of Olivers's hymn, which was inspired by a Hebrew song of praise, the *Yigdal* ("May he [God] be magnified"). The *Yigdal* is based on thirteen articles of Jewish faith codified in the twelfth century by Moses Maimonides and later paraphrased by Daniel ben Judah, a judge in Rome.

Thomas Olivers was a Welsh Wesleyan. Tradition has it that he wrote the hymn in 1770, after hearing the *Yigdal* sung by cantor Meyer Lyon and congregation at a London synagogue. Lyon is said to have given Olivers the tune, to which Olivers either freely adapted the *Yigdal* text or else wrote his own words, prompted by the tune and its Jewish associations. His hymn also echoes Revelation 4:9–11 and 5:6-14.[1]

Praise is rooted in wonder. Thomas Olivers conveys wonder with action verbs ("I bow and bless the sacred Name ") and by the attitude in which his hymn positions its singers. Ian Pitt-Watson's paraphrase of Psalm 139 invites a similar attitude:

> You are before me, Lord, you are behind,
>   and over me you have spread out your hand
> Such knowledge is too wonderful for me,
>   Too high to grasp, too great to understand.
>
> Then where, Lord, from your presence shall I go,
>   and from your Spirit where, Lord, shall I fly?
> If I ascend to heaven, you are there,
>   And still are with me if in hell I lie.
>
> If I should take my flight into the dawn,
>   or if I dwell on ocean's farthest shore,
> your mighty hand will rest upon me still,
>   and your right hand will guard me evermore.
>
> If I should say, "Let darkness cover me,
>   and I shall hide within the veil of night,"
> surely the darkness is not dark to you:
>   the night is as the day, the darkness light.
>
> Search me, O God, search me and know my heart.
>   Try me, O God, my mind and spirit try.
> Keep me from any path that gives you pain,
>   and lead me in the everlasting way.[2]

Copyright © 1973 by the Estate of Ian Pitt-Watson. All rights reserved. Used by permission.

The hymn renaissance has enlarged the vocabulary of Christian praise. Though some hymns retain Olivers's male-governance language of the Almighty King who reigns enthroned, a wider vocabulary has begun to emerge. From Deuteronomy 32:11, R. Deane Postlethwaite imagines God as an eagle caring for its young, following a number of translations that view the eagle (if it is an eagle) as female:

> The care the eagle gives her young,
>   safe in her lofty nest,
> is like the tender love of God
>   for us made manifest.
>
> As when the time to venture comes,
>   she stirs them out to flight,
> so we are pressed to boldly try,
>   to strive for daring height.
>
> And if we flutter helplessly,
>   as fledgling eagles fall,
> beneath us lift God's mighty wings
>   to bear us, one and all.[3]

Copyright © 1980 by Marjean Postlethwaite. All rights reserved. Used by permission.

My own hymn "Bring Many Names" recognizes that we name the Divine only indirectly, "in parable and story," then does so with a series of personal metaphors, biblically grounded and drawn from human experience:

> Strong mother God, working night and day,
> planning all the wonders of creation,
>   setting each equation, genius at play . . .
>
> Warm father God, hugging every child,
> feeling all the strains of human living,
>   caring and forgiving till we're reconciled . . .
>
> Old, aching God, grey with endless care,
> calmly piercing evil's new disguises,
>   glad of good surprises, wiser than despair . . .

Young, growing God, eager, on the move,
saying no to falsehood and unkindness,
   crying out for justice, giving all you have . . .

Great, living God, never fully known,
joyful darkness far beyond our seeing,
   closer yet than breathing, everlasting home . . .[4]

In a widely published hymn, Jaroslav Vajda uses only the title "God." But his vocabulary and syntax give multiple images of praise (full text, chapter 8). Vajda carefully arranges a series of vivid images. The opening sequence has an intergenerational appeal—sparrow, whale, and swirling stars. Later images invite reflection if one explores their Scripture sources (earthquake, storm, trumpet blast, prodigal, foe, pruning hook). The hymn appears to contain only questions, yet each question includes its response. In asking, *"How* does the creature say *Praise?"* the singer does cry "Praise!"—together with "Awe!" "Woe!" "Save!" "Grace!" "Thanks!" "Care!" "Life!" "Love!" "Peace!" "Joy!" and "Home!"[5]

Trinity

The *Yigdal* insists that God is One, in a Oneness that is unique, inscrutable, and infinite. As devout Jews, the first followers of Jesus-Messiah shared this impassioned monotheism. Yet from very early on they had three experiences of the One: the Holy Spirit, Jesus the Word made flesh, and the Divine Source from which the Word is sent. Reflection and controversy led to the conviction that this threefold experience cannot truthfully be collapsed into sameness nor divided into separateness. So Christian faith in its fullness is a *Trinitarian* monotheism, for which Thomas Olivers uses the traditional labels in their traditional sequence, "Father, Son, and Holy Ghost [Spirit]."[6]

The hymn renaissance offers several explorations of Trinitarian praise. Jeffery Rowthorn's "Creating God, Your Fingers Trace" includes three divine attributes (creating, redeeming, sustaining) plus a fourth:

Indwelling God, your gospel claims
one family with a billion names . . .[7]

Though some use "Creator, Redeemer, Sustainer" as equivalents of "Father, Son, and Holy Spirit," it is a mistake to treat them as job descriptions, because Trinitarian faith affirms that the whole Trinity creates, redeems, sustains, and indwells. Thus, Rowthorn's hymn fits into Trinitarian belief, but is not in a defined Trinitarian form.

By contrast, Thomas Troeger organizes forty scriptural metaphors in a Trinitarian sequence. His hymn can helpfully be read aloud by one or more voices, treating each image as an icon or stained-glass window to be savored. Some pairs are opposites, such as, "Judge—Defender," "Mercy—Might." Some sequences are gentle, others emphatic, such as, "Fountain, Shelter, Light" counterbalanced by "Thunder, Tempest, Whirlwind, Fire":

Source and Sovereign, Rock and Cloud,
    Fortress, Fountain, Shelter, Light,
Judge, Defender, Mercy, Might,
    Light whose life all life endowed . . .

Word and Wisdom, Root and Vine,
    Shepherd, Savior, Servant, Lamb,
Well and Water, Bread and Wine,
    Way who leads us to "I AM" . . .

Storm and Stillness, Breath and Dove,
    Thunder, Tempest, Whirlwind, Fire,
Comfort, Counselor, Presence, Love,
    Energies that never tire:
        May the church at prayer recall
        that no single, holy name
        but the truth that feeds them all
        is the God whom we proclaim.[8]

Copyright © Oxford University Press Inc., 1986. Reproduced by permission of Oxford University Press. All rights reserved.

Ruth Duck follows the traditional sequence of the Three, but begins, arrestingly, with "Womb" in place of "Father":

Womb of life, and source of being,
   home of every restless heart,
   in your arms the worlds awakened;
   you have loved us from the start . . .

Word in flesh, our brother Jesus,
   born to bring us second birth,
   you have come to stand beside us,
   knowing weakness, knowing earth . . .

Brooding Spirit, move among us;
   be our partner, be our friend.
   When our mem'ry fails, remind us
   whose we are, what we intend . . .

Mother, Brother, holy Partner;
   Father, Spirit, Only Son:
   we would praise your name forever,
   one-in-three, and three-in-one . . .[9]
           (Full text, chapter 8)

Carl Daw reverses the traditional sequence, effectively dislodging any subliminal impression that One of the Three is more important than the others:

God the Spirit, guide and guardian,
   wind-sped flame and hovering dove,
Breath of life and voice of prophets,
   sign of blessing, power of love . . .

Christ our Savior, sovereign, Shepherd,
   Word made flesh, love crucified,
      Teacher, healer, suffering servant,
       friend of sinners, foe of pride . . .

Great Creator, life bestower,
   truth beyond all thought's recall,
Fount of wisdom, womb of mercy,
   giving and forgiving all . . .

Triune God, mysterious being,
    undivided and diverse,
Deeper than our minds can fathom,
    greater than our creeds rehearse . . .[10]
        (Full text, chapter 8)

Jean Janzen takes a further step, praising the Three who are One in completely female imagery:

Mothering God, you gave me birth
    in the bright morning of this world.
Creator, source of every breath,
    you are my rain, my wind, my sun.

Mothering Christ, you took my form,
    offering me your food of light,
    grain of new life, and grape of love,
    your very body for my peace.

Mothering Spirit, nurturing one,
    in arms of patience hold me close,
    so that in faith I root and grow
until I flower, until I know.[11]

Copyright © 1991 by Jean Janzen, admin. by Augsburg Fortress. All rights reserved. Used by permission.

Amid Suffering and Sorrow

In the spirit of Thomas Olivers, we are called to praise God "though nature's strength decay, and earth and hell withstand" (oppose us). German Lutheran pastor and theologian Dietrich Bonhoeffer was imprisoned then executed in April 1945 for opposing the Nazi regime and joining a secret movement to overthrow it. One of his prison poems was translated by Fred Pratt Green, and appears in many hymnals:

By gracious powers so wonderfully sheltered,
    and confidently waiting, come what may,
we know that God is with us night and morning,
    and never fails to greet us each new day.

Yet is this heart by its old foe tormented,
    still evil days bring burdens hard to bear;
O give our frightened souls the sure salvation
    for which, O Lord, you taught us to prepare.

And when this cup you give is filled to brimming
    with bitter sorrow, hard to understand,
we take it thankfully and without trembling,
    out of so good and so beloved a hand.[12]

I don't have evidence, but surmise that publication of Pratt Green's translation has been influenced as much by the witness of Bonhoeffer's life as by the quality of Pratt Green's work. Biographies and discussions of Bonhoeffer are freely available on the Web. It would be interesting to know how far a new generation is aware of them, and how people who haven't heard of Bonhoeffer experience and interpret the hymn.

Fred Kaan (in a funeral hymn) and Bill Wallace invite us also to sing about "burdens hard to bear," and to trust the healing power of Christ suffering alongside us:

Lord of the living, in your name assembled
we join to thank you for the life remembered.
Father, have mercy, to your children giving
        hope in believing . . .

May we, whenever tempted to dejection,
strongly recapture thoughts of resurrection.
You gave us Jesus to defeat our sadness
        with Easter gladness.[13]

"Why has God forsaken me?"
    cried our Savior from the cross
as he shared the loneliness
    of our deepest grief and loss.

At the tomb of Lazarus
    Jesus wept with open grief.
Grant us, Lord, the tears which heal
    all our pain and unbelief.

As his life expired, our Lord
  placed himself within God's care.
At our dying, Lord, may we
  trust the love which conquers fear.

Mystery shrouds our life and death
  but we need not be afraid,
for the mystery's heart is love,
  God's great love which Christ displayed.[14]

Copyright © 1981 by Selah Publications. All rights reserved. Used by permission.

When clouds of suffering and loss finally roll away—in their own time, not in our culture's calendar of "closure"—we go on in praise:

This is a day of new beginnings,
time to remember, and move on,
time to believe what love is bringing,
laying to rest the pain that's gone . . .

Then let us, with the Spirit's daring,
step from the past, and leave behind
our disappointment, guilt and grieving,
seeking new paths, and sure to find.[15]

As I travel through the bad and good,
  keep me traveling the way I should;
where I see no way to go
  you'll be telling me the way, I know . . .

Give me courage when the world is rough,
  keep me loving though the world is tough;
leap and sing in all I do,
  keep me traveling along with you . . .

You are older than the world can be,
  you are younger than the life in me;
ever old and ever new,
  keep me traveling along with you:
    And it's from the old I travel to the new;
    keep me traveling along with you.[16]

Endless Praise

I believe, with the apostle Paul, that when we die our individual lives
perish utterly, and that no part of us survives: "Flesh and blood cannot
inherit the kingdom of God, nor does the perishable inherit the imper-
ishable" (1 Cor. 15:50). Anything "beyond" is a gift, not a given. I also
trust, with Paul, in God's power to bestow resurrection, so that with
Thomas Olivers we can hope to join the angels' endless praise. In a companion hymn to "Now," Jaroslav Vajda anticipates an ultimate "Then":

> Then the glory . . . the rest . . . the Sabbath peace unbroken . . .
> the garden . . . the throne . . . the crystal river flowing . . . the
> splendor . . . the life . . . the new creation singing . . . the mar-
> riage . . . the love . . . the feast of joy unending . . . the knowing
> . . . the light . . .the ultimate adventure . . . the Spirit's harvest
> gathered . . . the Lamb in majesty . . . the Father's Amen . . .
> Then . . . Then . . . Then.[17] (Full text of both hymns, chapter 8)

Natalie Sleeth's "Hymn of Promise" suggests that, just as we trust
that seeds will sprout and caterpillars turn into butterflies, we can trust
things as yet unrevealed, that only God can see:

> In the bulb there is a flower;
> in the seed, an apple tree;
> In cocoons, a hidden promise:
> butterflies will soon be free!
> In the cold and snow of winter
> there's a spring that waits to be,
> **unrevealed until its season,**
> **something God alone can see.**
>
> There's a song in every silence,
> seeking word and melody;
> There's a dawn in every darkness,
> bringing hope to you and me.
> From the past will come the future;
> what it holds, a mystery,
> **unrevealed until its season,**
> **something God alone can see.**

> In our end is our beginning;
>   in our time, infinity;
> In our doubt there is believing;
>   in our life, eternity;
> In our death, a resurrection;
>   at the last, a victory,
>   **unrevealed until its season,**
>   **something God alone can see.**[18]

Copyright © 1986 by Hope Publishing Company, Carol Stream, IL 60188. All rights reserved. Used by permission.

It is fitting to conclude with a song about praise, Fred Pratt Green's "When in Our Music God Is Glorified." When we wholeheartedly praise another, our attention is turned outward, not inward. Even more so, when our music glorifies God, "adoration leaves no room for pride." The hymn is carefully developed, with a repeated "Alleluia!" that itself encourages us fully to direct our praise to God. The repetition has subtle variations. The first "Alleluia" is what is sung ("as though the whole creation cried: Alleluia!"). Then it is variously the end of a sentence ("a more profound Alleluia!"), a response to a statement ("So has the Church . . . borne witness to the truth in every tongue, Alleluia!"), what is sung ("Then let us sing . . . Alleluia!"), and the end of the final sentence ("faith to sing always Alleluia!").

> When in our music God is glorified,
> and adoration leaves no room for pride,
> it is as though the whole creation cried: Alleluia!
>
> How often, making music, we have found
> a new dimension in the world of sound,
> as worship moved us to a more profound Alleluia!
>
> So has the Church, in liturgy and song,
> in faith and love, through centuries of wrong,
> borne witness to the truth in every tongue, Alleluia!
>
> And did not Jesus sing a psalm that night
> when utmost evil strove against the Light?
> Then let us sing, for whom he won the fight, Alleluia!

Let every instrument be tuned for praise!
Let all rejoice who have a voice to raise!
And may God give us faith to sing always Alleluia![19]

Copyright © 1972 by Hope Publishing Company, Carol Stream, IL 60188. All rights reserved. Used by permission.

To Do and Discuss

1. Pray with, use in worship, and explore the enlarged vocabulary of Christian praise (pp. 68–72).
2. Which of Tom Troeger's forty scriptural metaphors (p. 70) speak to you? Which don't? Why?
3. "Christian faith in its fullness is a *Trinitarian* monotheism" (p. 69). What does this mean? How can we practice it?
4. It has been said that there are Jesus Christians, Spirit Christians, and Father-Creator Christians, but there are very few Trinitarian Christians. Yes? No? Why?

Treasure

I have looked at a number of hymns from the English-language renaissance, highlighting their poetry and theology. Here, in conclusion, is a selection of hymns for use in prayer, discussion, meditation, and worship. For simplicity, I'll present them, as far as possible, in alphabetical order of first lines. This is a small selection, in order to keep this book to a manageable length. My choice is based on publication frequency and eloquence when read or spoken. If the text is printed or quoted in an earlier chapter, its publication statistics and copyright information are annotated there, so I give only the first line, author, and page reference.

The following hymns already printed in full form part of this treasury:

"Forgive Our Sins as We Forgive," by Rosamond Herklots (pp. 27–28)

"Give to Me, Lord, a Thankful Heart," by Thomas Caryl Micklem (pp. 61–62)

"In the Bulb There Is a Flower," by Natalie Sleeth (pp. 75–76)

"Jesu, Jesu," by Tom Colvin (pp. 41–42)

"Like the Murmur of the Dove's Song," by Carl P. Daw Jr. (pp. 18–19)

"Mothering God, You Gave Me Birth," by Jean Janzen (p. 72)

"Now Let Us from This Table Rise," by Fred Kaan (p. 44)

"O Day of Peace," by Carl P. Daw Jr. (p. 57)

"O Holy Spirit, Root of Life," by Jean Janzen (p. 22)

"Source and Sovereign, Rock and Cloud," by Thomas H. Troeger
(p. 70)
"Touch the Earth Lightly," by Shirley Erena Murray (p. 59)
"The Care the Eagle Gives Her Young," by R. Deane Postlethwaite
(p. 68)
"When in Our Music God Is Glorified," by Fred Pratt Green
(pp. 76–77)
"Why Has God Forsaken Me?" by William L. (Bill) Wallace
(pp. 73–74)
"You Are Before Me, Lord, You Are Behind," by Ian Pitt-Watson
(p. 67)

All Earth Is Waiting

All earth is waiting to see the Promised One,
   and open furrows await the seed of God.
   All the world, bound and struggling, seeks true liberty;
it cries out for justice and searches for the truth.

Thus says the prophet to those of Israel,
   "A virgin mother will bear Emmanuel."
   One whose name is "God with us," our Savior shall be,
through whom hope will blossom once more within our hearts.

All the rough places will turn to level ground,
   making new highways, new highways for our God,
   who is now coming closer, so come all and see,
and open the doorways as wide as can be.

In lowly stable the Promised One appeared,
   yet feel that presence throughout the earth today,
   For Christ lives in all Christians and comes to us now,
with peace and with justice to bring us liberty.

Alberto Taulé, trans. Gertrude Suppé

Translation copyright © 1989 by the United Methodist Publishing House, admin.
by the Copyright Company. All rights reserved. International copyright secured.
Used by permission.

An Upper Room Did Our Lord Prepare

An upper room did our Lord prepare
for those he loved until the end:
    and his disciples still gather there
    to celebrate their risen Friend.

A lasting gift Jesus gave his own,
to share his bread, his loving cup.
    Whatever burdens may bow us down,
    he by his cross shall lift us up.

And after supper he washed their feet,
for service, too, is sacrament.
    In him our joy shall be made complete
    sent out to serve, as he was sent.

No end there is! We depart in peace.
He loves beyond our uttermost:
    in every room in our Father's house
    he will be there, as Lord and host.

                                    Fred Pratt Green

Copyright © 1974 by Hope Publishing Company, Carol Stream, IL 60188. All rights reserved. Used by permission.

As a Chalice Cast of Gold

As a chalice cast of gold,
　　burnished, bright and brimmed with wine,
make me, Lord, as fit to hold
　　grace and truth and love divine.
　　　　Let my praise and worship start
　　　　with the cleansing of my heart.

Save me from the soothing sin
　　of the empty cultic deed
and the pious, babbling din
　　of the claimed but unlived creed.
　　　　Let my actions, Lord, express
　　　　what my tongue and lips profess.

When I bend upon my knees,
　　clasp my hands or bow my head,
let my spoken, public pleas
　　be directly, simply said,
　　　　free of tangled words that mask
　　　　what my soul would plainly ask.

When I dance or chant your praise,
　　when I sing a song or hymn,
when I preach your loving ways,
　　let my heart add its Amen.
　　　　Let each cherished, outward rite
　　　　thus reflect your inward light.

　　　　　　　　　　　Thomas H. Troeger

Copyright © Oxford University Press Inc. 1986. Reproduced by permission of Oxford University Press. All rights reserved.

Brother, Sister, Let Me Serve You

Brother, sister, let me serve you.
Let me be as Christ to you.
Pray that I might have the grace
to let you be my servant too.

We are pilgrims on a journey.
We are friends along the road.
We are here to help each other
walk the mile and bear the load.

I will hold the Christ-light for you
in the night time of your fear.
I will hold my hand out to you,
speak the peace you long to hear.

I will weep when you are weeping.
When you laugh I'll laugh with you.
I will share your joy and sorrow
'till we've seen this journey through.

When we sing to God in heaven
we shall find such harmony,
born of all we've known together
of Christ's love, and agony.

Brother, sister, let me serve you.
Let me be as Christ to you.
Pray that I might have the grace
to let you be my servant too.

Richard Gillard

Copyright © 1977 Scripture in Song/Maranatha Music/ASCAP (All rights administered by Music Services). All rights reserved. Used by permission.

Eternal Christ, You Rule

Eternal Christ, you rule,
keeping company with pain;
enduring ridicule,
    rejected, still you reign.

Eternal Christ, you rule,
speaking pardon from the cross;
forgiving pounding nails;
    death did its worst and lost.

Eternal Christ, you rule,
taking children by the hand;
the proud return to school;
    the meek receive the land.

Eternal Christ, you rule,
fasting forty days alone;
the tempter played the fool,
    expecting bread from stone.

Eternal Christ, you rule,
keeping company with pain;
with love and truth as tools,
    come build in us your reign.

                    Dan C. Damon

Copyright © 1991 by Hope Publishing Company, Carol Stream, IL 60188. All rights
reserved. Used by permission.

God Is Here

God is here! As we, God's people
    meet to offer praise and prayer,
may we find in fuller measure
    what it is in Christ we share.
Here, as in the world around us,
    all our varied skills and arts
wait the coming of the Spirit
    into open minds and hearts.

Here are symbols to remind us
    of our lifelong need of grace.
Here are table, font and pulpit.
    Here the cross has central place.
Here in honesty of preaching,
    here in silence, as in speech,
here in newness and renewal
    God the Spirit comes to each.

Here our children find a welcome
    in the Shepherd's flock and fold.
Here as bread and wine are taken,
    Christ sustains us as of old.
Here the servants of the Servant
    seek in worship to explore
what it means in daily living
    to believe and to adore.

God, our world is your dominion.
    In an age of change and doubt,
keep us faithful to the gospel;
    help us work your purpose out.
Here, in this day's dedication,
    all we have to give, receive;
we who cannot live without you,
    we adore you! We believe!

                                    Fred Pratt Green

Copyright © 1979 by Hope Publishing Company, Carol Stream, IL 60188. All rights reserved. Used by permission.

God of the Sparrow

God of the sparrow, God of the whale,
  God of the swirling stars,
    how does the creature say Awe?
    how does the creature say Praise?

God of the earthquake, God of the storm,
  God of the trumpet blast,
    how does the creature cry Woe?
    how does the creature cry Save?

God of the rainbow, God of the cross,
  God of the empty grave,
    how does the creature say Grace?
    how does the creature say Thanks?

God of the hungry, God of the sick,
  God of the prodigal,
    how does the creature say Care?
    how does the creature say Life?

God of the neighbor, God of the foe,
  God of the pruning hook,
    how does the creature say Love?
    how does the creature say Peace?

God of the ages, God near at hand,
  God of the loving heart,
    how do your children say Joy?
    how do your children say Home?
                              Jaroslav J. Vajda

Copyright © 1983 by Concordia Publishing House. Used by permission. All rights reserved.

God the Spirit, Guide and Guardian

God the Spirit, guide and guardian,
   wind-sped flame and hovering dove,
Breath of life and voice of prophets,
   sign of blessing, power of love,
give to those who lead your people,
   fresh anointing of your grace.
Send them forth as bold apostles
   to your church in every place.

Christ our Savior, sovereign, Shepherd,
   Word made flesh, love crucified,
teacher, healer, suffering servant,
   friend of sinners, foe of pride,
In your tending may all pastors
   learn and live a shepherd's care.
Grant them courage and compassion
   shown through word and deed and prayer.

Great Creator, life bestower,
   truth beyond all thought's recall,
fount of wisdom, womb of mercy,
   giving and forgiving all,
As you know our strength and weakness,
   so may those the church exalts
oversee its life steadfastly
   yet not overlook its faults.

Triune God, mysterious being,
   undivided and diverse,
deeper than our minds can fathom,
   greater than our creeds rehearse,
help us in our varied callings
   your full image to proclaim,
that our ministries uniting
   may give glory to your name.

Carl P. Daw Jr.

Copyright © 1989 by Hope Publishing Company, Carol Stream, IL 60188. All rights reserved. Used by permission.

Great God, Your Love Has Called Us Here

Great God, your love has called us here,
    as we, by love for love were made.
Your living likeness still we bear,
    though marred, dishonored, disobeyed.
        We come, with all our heart and mind
        your call to hear, your love to find.

We come with self-inflicted pains
    of broken trust and chosen wrong,
half-free, half-bound by inner chains,
    by social forces swept along,
        by powers and systems close confined,
        yet seeking hope for humankind.

Great God, in Christ you call our name
    and then receive us as your own,
not through some merit, right or claim,
    but by your gracious love alone.
        We strain to glimpse your mercy seat
        and find you kneeling at our feet.

Then take the towel, and break the bread,
    and humble us, and call us friends.
Suffer and serve till all are fed,
    and show how grandly love intends
        to work till all creation sings,
        to fill all worlds, to crown all things.

Great God, in Christ you set us free
    your life to live, your joy to share.
Give us your Spirit's liberty
    to turn from guilt and dull despair
        and offer all that faith can do
        while love is making all things new.

                              Brian Wren

Copyright © 1975, 1995 by Hope Publishing Company for the U.S.A., Canada, Australia, and New Zealand and by Strainer & Bell for all other territories. All rights reserved. Used by permission.

Here I Am, Lord

I, the Lord of sea and sky,
I have heard my people cry.
All who dwell in dark and sin
My hand will save.
I who made the stars of night,
I will make the darkness bright.
Who will bear my light to them? Whom shall I send?
  Here I am, Lord. Is it I, Lord?
  I have heard you calling in the night.
  I will go, Lord, if you lead me.
  I will hold your people in my heart.

I, the Lord of snow and rain,
I have borne my people's pain;
I have wept for love of them.
They turn away.
I will break their hearts of stone,
give them hearts for love alone.
I will speak my word to them. Whom shall I send?

I, the Lord of wind and flame,
I will tend the poor and lame.
I will set a feast for them.
My hand will save.
Finest bread I will provide
till their hearts are satisfied.
I will give my life for them. Whom shall I send?
  Here I am, Lord. Is it I, Lord?
  I have heard you calling in the night.
  I will go, Lord, if you lead me.
  I will hold your people in my heart.

Daniel Schutte

Text and music copyright © 1981 by O.C.P. Publications, 5536 N.E. Hassalo, Portland, OR 97213. All rights reserved. Used with permission.

Here in This Place (Gather Us In)

Here in this place, new light is streaming,
now is the darkness vanished away.
See, in this space, our fears and our dreamings,
brought here to you in the light of this day.
 Gather us in—the lost and forsaken,
 gather us in—the blind and the lame.
 Call to us now, and we shall awaken,
 we shall arise at the sound of our name.

We are the young—our lives are a mystery,
we are the old—who yearn for your face.
We have been sung throughout all of history,
called to be light to the whole human race.
 Gather us in—the rich and the haughty,
 gather us in—the proud and the strong.
 Give us a heart so meek and so lowly,
 give us the courage to enter the song.

Here we will take the wine and the water,
here we will take the bread of new birth.
Here you shall call your sons and your daughters,
call us anew to be salt for the earth.
 Give us to drink the wine of compassion,
 give us to eat the bread that is you.
 Nourish us well, and teach us to fashion
 lives that are holy and hearts that are true.

Not in the dark of buildings confining,
not in some heaven, light years away—
here in this place, the new light is shining;
now is the kingdom, now is the day.
 Gather us in and hold us forever,
 gather us in and make us your own.
 Gather us in—all peoples together,
 fire of love in our flesh and our bone.

Marty Haugen

Copyright © 1983 by G.I.A. Publications, Inc., 7404 S. Mason Ave., Chicago, IL 60638-3438. All rights reserved. Used by permission.

I Come with Joy

I come with joy, a child of God,
    forgiven, loved and free,
the life of Jesus to recall,
    in love laid down for me.

I come with Christians far and near
    to find, as all are fed,
the new community of love
    in Christ's communion bread.

As Christ breaks bread, and bids us share,
    each proud division ends.
The love that made us, makes us one,
    and strangers now are friends.

The Spirit of the risen Christ,
    unseen, but ever near,
is in such friendship better known,
    alive among us here.

Together met, together bound
    by all that God has done,
we'll go with joy, to give the world
    the love that makes us one.

Brian Wren

Copyright © 1969, 1982, 1994 by Hope Publishing Company for the U.S.A., Canada, Australia, and New Zealand and by Stainer & Bell for all other territories. All rights reserved. Used by permission.

Jesus Christ Is Waiting

Jesus Christ is waiting, waiting in the streets;
No one is his neighbor, all alone he eats.
Listen, Lord Jesus, I am lonely too.
Make me, friend or stranger,
fit to wait on you.

Jesus Christ is raging, raging in the streets,
where injustice spirals, and real hope retreats.
Listen, Lord Jesus, I am angry too.
In the kingdom's causes
let me rage with you.

Jesus Christ is healing, healing in the streets,
curing those who suffer, touching those he greets.
Listen, Lord Jesus, I have pity too.
Let my care be active,
healing just like you.

Jesus Christ is dancing, dancing in the streets,
where each sign of hatred he, with love, defeats.
Listen, Lord Jesus, I should triumph too.
On suspicion's graveyard
let me dance with you.

Jesus Christ is calling, calling in the streets,
"Who will join my journey? I will guide their feet."
Listen, Lord Jesus, let my fears be few.
Walk one step before me;
I will follow you.

John L. Bell and Graham Maule

Copyright © 1988 by Wild Goose Resource Group, Iona Community, Scotland. G.I.A. Publications, Inc., exclusive North American agent, 7404 S. Mason Ave., Chicago, IL 60638-3438. All rights reserved. Used by permission.

Lord, When You Came to the Seashore

Lord, when you came to the seashore,
you weren't seeking the wise or the wealthy,
but only asking that I might follow.
O Lord, in my eyes you were gazing.
Kindly smiling, my name you were saying.
All I treasured, I have left on the sand there.
Close to you, I will find other seas.

Lord, you knew what my boat carried:
  neither money nor weapons for fighting,
    but nets for fishing, my daily labor.

Lord, have you need of my labor,
hands for service, a heart made for loving,
my arms for lifting the poor and broken?

Lord, send me where you would have me:
To a village, or heart of the city.
I will remember that you are with me.
O Lord, in my eyes you were gazing.
Kindly smiling, my name you were saying.
All I treasured, I have left on the sand there.
Close to you, I will find other seas.

Spanish text and music copyright © 1979 by Cesáreo Gabaráin. Published by O.C.P.
Publications, 5536 N.E. Hassalo, Portland, OR 97213. English text copyright ©
1982 by Willard F. Jabusch (admin. by O.C.P. Publications). All rights reserved.
Used with permission.

Lord, Whose Love in Humble Service

Lord, whose love in humble service
   bore the weight of human need,
who upon the Cross, forsaken,
   worked your mercy's perfect deed:
we, your servants, bring the worship
   not of voice alone, but heart;
consecrating to your purpose
   every gift that you impart.

Still your children wander homeless;
   still the hungry cry for bread;
still the captives long for freedom;
   still in grief we mourn our dead.
As you, Lord, in deep compassion
   healed the sick and freed the soul,
use the love your Spirit kindles,
   saving, healing, making whole.

As we worship, grant us vision,
   till your love's revealing light,
in its height and depth and greatness
   dawns upon our wakened[1] sight;
making known the needs and burdens
   your compassion bids us bear,
stirring us to tireless striving
   your abundant life to share.

Called from worship unto service,
   forth in your dear name we go,
to the child, the youth, the aged,
   love in living deeds to show.
Hope and health, goodwill and comfort,
   counsel, aid and peace we'll give,
that your children, Lord, in freedom
   may your mercy know, and live.

            Albert F. Bayly (1901–84)

Copyright © 1988 Oxford University Press. Reproduced by permission. All rights reserved.

Now Join We to Praise the Creator

Now join we, to praise the Creator,
  our voices in worship and song;
We stand to recall with thanksgiving
  that to God all seasons belong.

We thank you, O God, for your goodness,
  for the joy and abundance of crops,
for food that is stored in our larders,
  for all we can buy in the shops.

But also of need and starvation
  we sing with concern and despair,
of skills that are used for destruction,
  of land that is burnt and laid bare.

We cry for the plight of the hungry
  while harvests are left on the field,
for orchards neglected and wasting,
  for produce from markets withheld.

The song grows in depth and in wideness;
  the earth and its people are one.
There can be no thanks without giving,
  no words without deeds that are done.

Then teach us, O God of the harvest,
  to be humble in all that we claim,
to share what we have with the nations,
  to care for the world in your name.

                                      Fred Kaan

Copyright © 1989 by Hope Publishing Company for the U.S.A., Canada, Australia, and New Zealand and by Stainer & Bell for all other territories. All rights reserved. Used by permission.

Now the Silence

Now the silence
Now the peace
Now the empty hands uplifted
Now the kneeling
Now the plea
Now the Father's arms in
  welcome
Now the hearing
Now the power
Now the vessel brimmed for
  pouring
Now the body
Now the blood
Now the joyful celebration
Now the wedding
Now the songs
Now the heart forgiven leaping
Now the Spirit's visitation
Now the Son's epiphany
Now the Father's blessing
  Now
    Now
      Now

Then the Glory

Then the glory
Then the rest
Then the Sabbath peace
  unbroken
Then the garden
Then the throne
Then the crystal river flowing
Then the splendor
Then the life
Then the new creation singing
Then the marriage
Then the love
Then the feast of joy unending
Then the knowing
Then the light
Then the ultimate adventure
Then the Spirit's harvest
  gathered
Then the Lamb in majesty
Then the Father's Amen
  Then
    Then
      Then

Jaroslav Vajda

Copyright © 1969 by Hope Publishing Company, Carol Stream, IL 60188. All rights reserved. Used by permission.

O for a World

O for a world where everyone
    respects each other's ways,
where love is lived and all is done
    with justice and with praise.

O for a world where goods are shared
    and misery relieved,
where truth is spoken, children spared,
    equality achieved.

We welcome one world family
    and struggle with each choice
that opens us to unity
    and gives our vision voice.

The poor are rich, the weak are strong,
    the foolish ones are wise.
Tell all who mourn: outcasts belong,
    who perishes will rise.

O for a world preparing for
    God's glorious reign of peace,
where time and tears will be no more
    and all but love will cease.

Miriam Therese Winter

Copyright © 1987 by Medical Mission Sisters. All rights reserved. Used by permission.

O God of Every Nation

O God of every nation,
    of every race and land,
redeem the whole creation
    with your almighty hand;
where hate and fear divide us
    and bitter threats are hurled,
in love and mercy guide us
    and heal our strife-torn world.

From search for wealth and power
    and scorn of truth and right,
from trust in bombs that shower
    destruction through the night,
from pride of race and nation
    and blindness to your way,
deliver every nation,
    eternal God, we pray!

Lord, strengthen all who labor
    that we may find release
from fear of rattling saber,
    from dread of war's increase;
when hope and courage falter,
    your still small voice be heard;
with faith that none can alter,
    your servants undergird.

Keep bright in us the vision
    of days when war shall cease,
when hatred and division
    give way to love and peace,
till dawns the morning glorious
    when truth and justice reign
and Christ shall rule victorious
    o'er all the world's domain.
                    William Watkins Reid Jr.

Copyright © 1958 renewed 1986 by the Hymn Society in the U.S. and Canada
(admin. by Hope Publishing Company, Carol Stream, IL 60188). All rights reserved.
Used by permission.

O God, We Bear the Imprint of Your Face

O God, we bear the imprint of your face:
  the colors of our skin are your design,
and what we have of beauty in our race
  as man or woman, you alone define,
    who stretched a living fabric on our frame
    and gave to each a language and a name.

Where we are torn and pulled apart by hate
  because our race, our skin is not the same,
while we are judged unequal by the state
  and victims made because we own our name,
    humanity reduced to little worth,
    dishonored is your living face on earth.

O God, we share the image of your Son
  whose flesh and blood are ours, whatever skin;
in his humanity we find our own,
  and in his family our proper kin:
    Christ is the brother we still crucify,
    his love the language we must learn, or die.

                    Shirley Erena Murray

Copyright © 1987 by Hope Publishing Company, Carol Stream, IL 60188. All rights reserved. Used by permission.

O Praise the Gracious Power

O praise the gracious power
that tumbles walls of fear
and gathers in one house of faith
all strangers far and near:
We praise you Christ!
Your cross has made us one!

O praise persistent truth
that opens fisted minds
and eases from their anxious clutch
the prejudice that binds:

O praise inclusive love
encircling every race,
oblivious to gender, wealth,
to social rank or place:

O praise the word of faith
that claims us as God's own,
a living temple built on Christ,
our rock and corner stone:

O praise the tide of grace
that laps at every shore
with visions of a world at peace
no longer bled by war:

O praise the power, the truth,
the love, the word, the tide.
Yet more than these, O praise their source,
praise Christ, the crucified:

O praise the living Christ
with faith's bright songful voice!
Announce the gospel to the world
and with these words rejoice:
We praise you Christ!
Your cross has made us one!
Thomas H. Troeger

Copyright © Oxford University Press Inc. 1986. Reproduced by permission of Oxford University Press. All rights reserved.

One Bread, One Body

One bread, one body, one Lord of all,
one cup of blessing which we bless.
And we, though many, throughout the earth,
we are one body in this one Lord.
Gentile or Jew, servant or free,
  woman or man, no more.

  Many the gifts, many the works,
  one in the Lord of all.

  Grain for the fields, scattered and grown,
  gathered to one, for all.
One bread, one body, one Lord of all,
one cup of blessing which we bless.
And we, though many, throughout the earth,
we are one body in this one Lord.
John B. Foley, S.J.

Copyright © 1978 by John B. Foley, SJ, published by O.C.P. Publications, 5536 N.E. Hassalo, Portland, OR 97213. All rights reserved. Used with permission.

Put Peace into Each Other's Hands

Put peace into each other's hands
and like a treasure hold it.
Protect it like a candle flame,
with tenderness enfold it.

Put peace into each other's hands
with loving expectation.
Be gentle in your words and ways,
in touch with God's creation.

Put peace into each other's hands
like bread we break for sharing.
Look people warmly in the eye:
Our life is meant for caring.

As at communion, shape your hands
into a waiting cradle.
The gift of Christ receive, revere,
united round the table.

Put Christ into each other's hands;
he is love's deepest measure.
In love make peace, give peace a chance,
and share it like a treasure.

Fred Kaan

Copyright © 1989 by Hope Publishing Company, Carol Stream, IL 60188. All rights reserved. Used by permission.

Silence! Frenzied, Unclean Spirit!

"Silence! Frenzied, unclean spirit,"
 cried God's healing, holy One.
"Cease your ranting! Flesh can't bear it.
 Flee as night before the sun."
At Christ's voice the demon trembled,
  from its victim madly rushed,
    while the crowd that was assembled
    stood in wonder, stunned and hushed.

Lord, the demons still are thriving
  in the grey cells of the mind:
tyrant voices shrill and driving,
  twisted thoughts that grip and bind,
doubts that stir the heart to panic,
  fears distorting reason's sight,
    guilt that makes our loving frantic,
    dreams that cloud the soul with fright.

Silence, Lord, the unclean spirit
  in our mind and in our heart.
Speak your word that when we hear it,
  all our demons shall depart.
Clear our thought and calm our feeling,
  still the fractured, warring soul.
    By the power of your healing
    make us faithful, true and whole.

                              Thomas H. Troeger

Copyright © Oxford University Press Inc. 1984. Reproduced by permission of Oxford University Press. All rights reserved.

Spirit

**Spirit, Spirit of gentleness, blow through the wilderness,
   calling and free.
Spirit, Spirit of restlessness, stir me from placidness,
   wind on the sea.**

You moved on the waters.
   You called to the deep,
then you coaxed up the mountains
   from the valleys of sleep,
and over the eons
   you called to each thing:
"Awake from your slumbers
   and rise on your wings!"

You swept through the desert,
   you stung with the sand,
and you gifted your people
   with a law and a land,
and when they were blinded
   with their idols and lies,
then you spoke through your prophets
   to open their eyes.

You sang in a stable,
   you cried from a hill,
then you whispered in silence
   when the whole world was still,
and down in the city
   you called once again,
when you blew through your people
   on the rush of the wind.

You call from tomorrow.
   You break ancient schemes.
From the bondage of sorrow
   the captives dream dreams.
Our women see visions.
   Our men clear their eyes.

With bold new decisions
   your people arise.

**Spirit, Spirit of gentleness, blow through the wilderness,
   calling and free.
Spirit, Spirit of restlessness, stir me from placidness,
   wind on the sea.**

James K. Manley

Words and music copyright © 1978 by James K. Manley. Used by permission.

There's a Spirit in the Air

There's a spirit in the air,
telling Christians everywhere:
   "Praise the love that Christ revealed,
   living, working in our world!"

Lose your shyness, find your tongue,
tell the world what God has done:
   God in Christ has come to stay.
   Live tomorrow's life today!

When believers break the bread,
when a hungry child is fed,
   praise the love that Christ revealed,
   living, working, in our world.

Still the Spirit gives us light,
seeing wrong and setting right:
   God in Christ has come to stay.
   Live tomorrow's life today!

When a stranger's not alone,
where the homeless find a home,
   praise the love that Christ revealed,
   living, working, in our world.

May the Spirit fill our praise,
guide our thoughts and change our ways.
   God in Christ has come to stay.
   Live tomorrow's life today!

There's a Spirit in the air,
calling people everywhere:
   Praise the love that Christ revealed,
   living, working, in our world.
Brian Wren

Copyright © 1969, 1995 by Hope Publishing Company for the U.S.A., Canada, Australia, and New Zealand and by Stainer & Bell for all other territories. All rights reserved. Used by permission.

These Things Did Thomas Count as Real

These things did Thomas count as real:
the warmth of blood, the chill of steel,
the grain of wood, the heft of stone,
the last frail twitch of flesh and bone.

The vision of his skeptic mind
was keen enough to make him blind
to any unexpected act
too large for his small world of fact.

His reasoned certainties denied
that one could live when one had died,
until his fingers read like braille
the markings of the spear and nail.

May we, O God, by grace believe,
and thus the risen Christ receive,
whose raw imprinted palms reached out
and beckoned Thomas from his doubt.

Thomas H. Troeger

Copyright © Oxford University Press Inc. 1986. Reproduced by permission of
Oxford University Press. All rights reserved.

Touch the Earth Lightly

Touch the earth lightly,
use the earth gently,
nourish the life of the world in our care:
gift of great wonder,
ours to surrender,
trust for the children tomorrow will bear.

We who endanger,
who create hunger,
agents of death for all creatures that live,
we who would foster
clouds of disaster,
God of our planet, forestall and forgive!

Let there be greening,
birth from the burning,
water that blesses and air that is sweet,
health in God's garden,
hope in God's children,
regeneration that peace will complete.

God of all living,
God of all loving,
God of the seedling, the snow, and the sun,
teach us, deflect us,
Christ, reconnect us,
using us gently, and making us one.

Shirley Erena Murray

Copyright © 1992 by Hope Publishing Company, Carol Stream, IL 60188. All rights reserved. Used by permission.

What Does the Lord Require?

What does the Lord require
  for praise and offering?
What sacrifice, desire
  or tribute bid you bring?
Do justly!
  Love mercy!
    Walk humbly with your God!

Rulers of earth, give ear!
  Should you not justice know?
Will God your pleading hear,
  while crime and cruelty grow?
Do justly!
  Love mercy!
    Walk humbly with your God!

Leaders in wealth and trade,
  for whom the workers toil,
think not to win God's aid
  if lies your commerce soil.
Do justly!
  Love mercy!
    Walk humbly with your God!

Still down the ages ring
  the prophet's stern commands:
to merchant, worker, king,
  he brings God's high demands.
Do justly!
  Love mercy!
    Walk humbly with your God!

How shall our life fulfill
  God's law so hard and high?
Let Christ endue our will
  with grace to fortify.
Then justly,
  in mercy,
    we'll humbly walk with God.
Albert Frederick Bayly (1901–84)

Copyright © 1988 Oxford University Press. Reproduced by permission. All rights reserved.

What Is This Place Where We Are Meeting?

What is this place where we are meeting?
Only a house, the earth its floor,
walls and a roof sheltering people,
windows for light, an open door.
    Yet it becomes a body that lives
        when we are gathered here,
        and know our God is near.

Words from afar, stars that are falling,
sparks that are sown in us like seed:
names for our God, dreams, signs and wonders
sent from the past are all we need.
    We in this place remember and speak
        again what we have heard:
        God's free redeeming word.

And we accept bread at this table,
broken and shared, a living sign.
Here in this world, dying and living,
we are each other's bread and wine.
    This is the place where we can receive
        what we need to increase:
        our justice and God's peace.

                                Huub Osterhuis

Text and arrangement copyright © 1967, Gooi en Sticht, BV., Baarn, The Netherlands. All rights reserved. Exclusive agent for English-language countries: O.C.P. Publications, 5536 N.E. Hassalo, Portland, OR 97213. All rights reserved. Used with permission.

When Love Is Found
(A Hymn about Lifetime Partnership)

When love is found
  and hope comes home,
    sing and be glad
      that two are one.
      When love explodes
  and fills the sky,
  praise God, and share
our Maker's joy.

When love has flowered
  in trust and care,
    build both each day,
      that love may dare
      to reach beyond
  home's warmth and light,
  to serve and strive
for truth and right.

When love is tried
  as loved-ones change,
    hold still to hope,
      though all seems strange,
      till ease returns
  and love grows wise
  through listening ears
and opened eyes.

When love is torn,
  and trust betrayed,
    pray strength to love
      till torments fade,
      till lovers keep
  no score of wrong,
  but hear through pain
love's Easter song.

Praise God for love,
praise God for life,
in age or youth,
in calm or strife.
Lift up your hearts!
Let love be fed
through death and life
in wine and bread.

Brian Wren

Copyright © 1983 by Hope Publishing Company for the U.S.A., Canada, Australia, and New Zealand and by Stainer & Bell for all other territories. All rights reserved. Used by permission.

When the Poor Ones

When the poor ones who have nothing still are giving;
   when the thirsty pass the cup, water to share;
   when the wounded offer others strength and healing:
we see God, here by our side, walking our way.

When compassion gives the suffering consolation;
   when expecting brings to birth hope that was lost;
   when we choose love, not the hatred all around us:
we see God, here by our side, walking our way.

When our spirits, like a chalice, brim with gladness;
   when our voices, full and clear, sing out the truth;
   when our longings, free from envy, seek the humble:
we see God, here by our side, walking our way.

When the goodness poured from heaven fills our dwellings;
   when the nations work to change war into peace;
   when the stranger is accepted as our neighbor:
we see God, here by our side, walking our way.

José Antonio Olivar, trans. Martin A. Seltz

Copyright © 1971 by J. A. Olivar, Miguel Manzano & San Pablo Internacional–SSP. Sole U.S. agent and publisher, O.C.P. Publications, Inc., 5536 N.E. Hassalo, Portland, OR 97213. All rights reserved. Used with permission.

Will You Come and Follow Me
(The Summons)

Will you come and follow me if I but call your name?
Will you go where you don't know and never be the same?
Will you let my love be shown? Will you let my name be known?
Will you let my life be grown in you and you in me?

Will you leave yourself behind if I but call your name?
Will you care for cruel and kind and never be the same?
Will you risk the hostile stare should your life attract or scare?
Will you let me answer prayer in you and you in me?

Will you let the blinded see if I but call your name?
Will you set the prisoners free and never be the same?
Will you kiss the leper clean and do such as this unseen,
and admit to what I mean in you and you in me?

Will you love the "you" you hide if I but call your name?
Will you quell the fear inside and never be the same?
Will you use the faith you've found to reshape the world around,
through my sight and touch and sound in you and you in me?

Lord, your summons echoes true when you but call my name.
Let me turn and follow you and never be the same.
In your company I'll go where your love and footsteps show.
Thus I'll move and live and grow in you and you in me.

John L. Bell and Graham Maule

Copyright © 1987, 1995, 2000 by Wild Goose Resource Group, Iona Community, Scotland. G.I.A. Publications, Inc., exclusive North American agent, 7404 S. Mason Ave., Chicago, IL 60638-3438. All rights reserved. Used by permission.

Wind Who Makes All Winds That Blow

Wind who makes all winds that blow—
  gusts that bend the saplings low,
    gales that heave the sea in waves,
      stirrings in the mind's deep caves—
    aim your breath with steady power
  on your church, this day, this hour.
Raise, renew the life we've lost,
Spirit God of Pentecost!

Fire who fuels all fires that burn—
  suns around which planets turn,
    beacons marking reefs and shoals,
      shining truth to guide our souls—
    come to us as once you came:
  burst in tongues of sacred flame!
Light and Power, Might and Strength,
fill your church, its breadth and length.

Holy Spirit, Wind and Flame,
  move within our mortal frame.
    Make our hearts an altar pyre.
      Kindle them with your own fire.
    Breathe and blow upon that blaze
  till our lives, our deeds and ways
speak that tongue which every land
by your grace shall understand.

                    Thomas H. Troeger

Copyright © Oxford University Press Inc. 1986. Reproduced by permission of Oxford University Press. All rights reserved.

Womb of Life, and Source of Being

Womb of life, and source of being,
   home of every restless heart,
in your arms the worlds awakened;
   you have loved us from the start.
We, your children, gather round you,
   at the table you prepare.
      Sharing stories, tears, and laughter,
      we are nurtured by your care.

Word in flesh, our brother Jesus,
   born to bring us second birth,
you have come to stand beside us,
   knowing weakness, knowing earth.
Priest who shares our human struggles,
   Life of Life, and Death of Death,
      risen Christ, come stand among us,
      send the Spirit by your breath.

Brooding Spirit, move among us;
   be our partner, be our friend.
When our mem'ry fails, remind us
   whose we are, what we intend.
Labor with us, aid the birthing
   of the new world yet to be,
      free of servant, lord, and master,
      free for love and unity.

Mother, Brother, holy Partner;
   Father, Spirit, Only Son:
we would praise your name forever,
   one-in-three, and three-in-one.
We would share your life, your passion,
   share your word of world made new,
      ever singing, ever praising,
      one with all, and one with you.

Ruth Duck

Copyright © 1992 by G.I.A. Publications, Inc., 7404 S. Mason Ave., Chicago, IL 60638-3438. All rights reserved. Used by permission.

You Satisfy the Hungry Heart

**You satisfy the hungry heart
with gift of finest wheat.
Come give to us, O saving Lord,
the bread of life to eat.**

As when the shepherd calls his sheep,
they know and heed his voice;
so when you call your family, Lord,
we follow and rejoice.

With joyful lips we sing to you
our praise and gratitude
that you should count us worthy, Lord,
to share this heavenly food.

Is not the cup we bless and share
the blood of Christ outpoured?
Do not one cup, one loaf declare
our oneness in one Lord?

The mystery of your presence, Lord,
no mortal tongue can tell:
whom all the world cannot contain
comes in our hearts to dwell.

You give yourself to us, O Lord,
then selfless let us be,
to serve each other in your name
in truth and charity.

**You satisfy the hungry heart
with gift of finest wheat,
come give to us, O saving Lord,
the bread of life to eat.**

Omer Westendorf

Copyright permission obtained, Archdiocese of Philadelphia, 1977. All rights reserved.

To Do and Discuss

1. Use one or more hymns in this chapter for prayer, conversation, or meditation.
2. How many hymns in this chapter have you heard or sung? Which, if any, would you now like to sing? (Remember to get permission.)
3. How old is your church's hymnal—if it has one? When is it time to get a new hymnal?

Hymnal Sources (1983–2007)

The publication year is followed by title, abbreviation (in parentheses), denomination, and country. In the notes, hymnal abbreviations are in chronological order, not alphabetical order. The Roman Catholic Church has no officially authorized hymnal. In North America, G.I.A. Publications, Inc., is widely used and is my semiofficial choice. In Australia, Roman Catholics and Protestants jointly published *Together in Song*.

1983	*Hymns Ancient & Modern New Standard*	(AMNS)	Church of England	U.K.
1983	*Hymns and Psalms*	(HPS)	Methodist	U.K.
1985	*Rejoice in the Lord*	(RITL)	Reformed Church in America	U.S.A.
1985	*The Hymnal 1982*	(H82)	Episcopal Church	U.S.A.
1987	*Psalter Hymnal*	(PSH)	Christian Reformed Church	U.S.A.
1989	*The United Methodist Hymnal*	(UMH)	United Methodist Church	U.S.A.
1990	*The Presbyterian Hymnal*	(PH)	Presbyterian Church (U.S.A.)	U.S.A.
1991	*The Baptist Hymnal*	(BH)	Southern Baptist	U.S.A.
1991	*Baptist Praise and Worship*	(BPW)	Baptist	U.K.

1991	*Rejoice and Sing*	(RJS)	United Reformed Church	U.K.
1992	*Hymnal—A Worship Book*	(HWB)	Mennonite/Church of the Brethren	U.S.A.
1993	*Alleluia Aotearoa*	(AA)	New Zealand Hymnbook Trust	New Zealand/ Aotearoa
1995	*Chalice Hymnal*	(CH)	Disciples of Christ	U.S.A.
1995	*The New Century Hymnal*	(NCH)	United Church of Christ	U.S.A.
1996	*Ritual Song*	(RSG)	Roman Catholic (G.I.A.)	U.S.A.
1996	*Voices United*	(VU)	United Church of Canada	Canada
1997	*The Book of Praise*	(BPR)	Presbyterian Church in Canada	Canada
1999	*Together in Song: Australian Hymn Book II*	(AHB)	Multidenominational	Australia
2000	*The Faith We Sing*	(TFWS)	United Methodist Church	U.S.A.
2001	*Worship III*	(WP3)	Roman Catholic (G.I.A.)	U.S.A.
2005	*Church Hymnary*: Fourth Edition	(CH4)	Church of Scotland	U.K.
2006	*Evangelical Lutheran Worship*	(ELW)	Evangelical Lutheran Church in America	U.S.A.
2007	*More Voices*	(MV)	United Church of Canada	Canada

Notes

All items in copyright are used by permission of the copyright owner or controller, all of whose rights are reserved.

Chapter 1: Hymns?—For Today?

1. From "When I Survey the Wondrous Cross." Watts can be graphic as well as restrained. The following stanza, often omitted, begins "His dying crimson, like a robe, / spreads o'er his body on the tree."
2. From Thomas H. Troeger [*Troh*-ger], "These Things Did Thomas Count as Real." PSH 394, NCH 254, AHB 649. Copyright © 1986 by Oxford University Press, Inc.
3. A more complete discussion of hymn form and structure is in Brian Wren, *Praying Twice: The Music and Words of Congregational Song* (Louisville, KY: Westminster John Knox Press, 2000), chap. 8.
4. I say *poetic* meter because the word *meter* sometimes also denotes the rhythmic pulse or "beat" in a piece of music (often called its *time* or *time signature*). Though the rhythms of speech and music sometimes coincide, their priorities and rhythmic systems are distinct and different.
5. Quoted from "The King of Love My Shepherd Is" (Henry Williams Baker (1821–77) and "Glorious Things of Thee Are Spoken" (John Newton, 1725–1807).
6. In the 23 hymnals surveyed, my main sources are 30 hymns published five times, 21 six times, 15 seven times, 22 eight times, and 27 published ten times or more.

Chapter 2: Jesus

1. From "You, Lord, Are Both Lamb and Shepherd" (subtitled *Christus Paradox*), by Sylvia G. Dunstan: VU 210, RSG 699,

BPR 356, CH4 355, TFWS 2102. Copyright 1991 by G.I.A. Publications, Inc.

2. From "We Know that Christ Is Raised and Dies No More," by John Brownlow Geyer (b. 1932): RITL 528, H82 296, PSH 271, UMH 610, PH 495, RJS 426, CH 376, RSG 906, VU 448, BPR 522, AHB 489, WP3 721, CH4 635, ELW 449. Author's copyright.

3. From "Christ Is Alive!" by Brian Wren: HPS 190, H82 182, PSH 413, UMH 318, PH 108, BH 173, BPW 244, RJS 260, HWB 278, RSG 601, VU 158, BPR 251, AHB 387, WP3 466, CH4 416, ELW 389. Written April 1968, revised 1978, 1989, 1993. Copyright © 1975 by Hope Publishing Company for the U.S.A., Canada, Australia, and New Zealand, and by Stainer & Bell for all other territories.

4. From "Eternal Christ, You Rule," by Dan C. Damon: NCH 302, VU 212. Copyright © 1991 by Hope Publishing Company, Carol Stream, IL 60188.

5. From "Morning Glory, Starlit Sky," by William H. Vanstone (1923–99). AMNS 496, RITL 351, H82 585, UMH 194, RJS 99, AHB 174, CH4 390. (CH4 begins at "Open are the gifts of God") Copyright © William H. Vanstone estate. Reproduced by permission.

6. African American slave song: AMNS 523, HPS 181, H82 172, PSH 377, UMH 288, PH 102, BH 156, RJS 227, HWB 257, CH 198, NCH 229, RSG 570, VU 144, BPR 233, AHB 345, WP3 436, CH4 403, ELW 353. Words and melody are in the public domain (so freely available) but be aware that many arrangements are copyrighted.

7. From "Blessed Be the God of Israel," by Michael Perry: H82 444, UMH 209, CH 135, VU 901 ("Blest"), BPR 752 ("Blest"), ELW 552. Copyright © 1973 by Hope Publishing Company, Carol Stream, IL 60188.

8. From "All Earth Is Waiting," by Alberto Taulé (trans. Gertrude Suppé): UMH 210, CH 139, VU 5, BPR 109. Translation copyright © 1989 by the United Methodist Publishing House, administered by the Copyright Company. ELW 266 has a different translation.

9. The phrase "Magnificat anima mea Dominum" (My soul glorifies the Lord) begins the Latin version of this song.

10. From "My Soul Gives Glory to My God," by Miriam Therese Winter: UMH 198, CH 130, NCH 119, VU 899, BPR 123, AHB 172. Copyright © 1987 by Medical Mission Sisters.

11. From "Tell Out, My Soul, the Greatness of the Lord!" by Timothy Dudley-Smith: AMNS 422, HPS 86, RITL 182, H82 437 and 438, PSH 478, UMH 200, BH 81, BPW 391, RJS 740, AHB 161, WP3 534, CH4 286. Copyright © 1962, renewed 1990, by Hope Publishing Company, Carol Stream, IL 60188. This hymn appears in many other hymnals and song collections.

12. From "When Jesus Came to Jordan," by Fred Pratt Green: AMNS 526, HPS 132, UMH 252, PH 72, RSG 878, WP3 697, ELW 305.

Copyright © 1980 by Hope Publishing Company, Carol Stream, IL 60188.

13. From "Silence! Frenzied, Unclean Spirit!" by Thomas H. Troeger: UMH 264, HWB 630, CH 186, NCH 176, VU 620, BPR 729, WP3 751. Copyright © 1984 by Oxford University Press, Inc.

14. From "An Upper Room Did Our Lord Prepare," by Fred Pratt Green: AMNS 434, HPS 594, RITL 568, PH 94, BPW 429, RJS 438, CH 385, VU 130, BPR 224, AHB 536. Copyright © 1974 by Hope Publishing Company, Carol Stream, IL 60188.

15. From "Woman in the Night," by Brian Wren: UMH 274, CH 188, BPR 657, AHB 661. Copyright © 1983, 1995 by Hope Publishing Company for the U.S.A., Canada, Australia, and New Zealand, and by Stainer & Bell for all other territories. Scripture sources for the stanzas quoted are Mark 5:24–34; John 4:7–30; Luke 7:36–50; Luke 8:1–3; John 19:25; and Luke 23:55–24:10.

16. From "I Danced in the Morning" (Lord of the Dance), by Sydney B. Carter (1915–2004): AMNS 375,UMH 261, PH 302, RJS 195, RSG 809, VU 352, BPR 250, AHB 242, WP3 636, CH4 404. Copyright © 1963 by Hope Publishing Company for the U.S.A., Canada, Australia, and New Zealand, and by Stainer & Bell for all other territories. The medieval carol is "Tomorrow Shall Be My Dancing Day."

17. From "Who Would Think that What Was Needed?" by John Bell and Graham Maule: RJS 178, NCH 143, CH4 295. Copyright © 1990 by Wild Goose Resource Group, Iona Community, Scotland. G.I.A. Publications, Inc., exclusive North American agent.

Chapter 3: Spirit

1. The act of anointing with oil.

2. The "sevenfold gifts" are taken loosely from Isaiah 11:1–10, especially vv. 2–3. In Roman Catholic tradition they are (in one modern interpretation): Wisdom—to discern God's will; Understanding—to make good decisions; Fortitude—courage to do the right thing; Knowledge—leading us to wisdom and understanding; Piety; Reverence; and Wonder / Awe.

3. From "Filled with the Spirit's Power with One Accord," by J. R. Peacey (1896–1971): AMNS 359, HPS 314, RITL 373, PSH 417, UMH 537, HWB 289, NCH 266, VU 194, BPR 282, AHB 411. Copyright © 1978 by Hope Publishing Company, Carol Stream, IL 60188.

4. From "Wind Who Makes All Winds That Blow," by Thomas. H. Troeger: UMH 538, PH 131, CH 236, NCH 271, VU 196, BPR 281. Copyright © 1983, 1985 by Oxford University Press, Inc.

5. "Like the Murmur of the Dove's Song," by Carl P. Daw Jr : H82 513, UMH 544, PH 314, HWB 29, CH 245, NCH 270, VU 205, BPR 385,

AHB 419, CH4 592, ELW 403. Copyright © 1982 by Hope Publishing Company, Carol Stream, IL 60188.

6. From "Loving Spirit," by Shirley Erena Murray: PH 323, RJS 326, AA 94, CH 244, VU 387, AHB 417, TFWS 2123, CH4 597, ELW 397. Copyright © 1987 The Hymn Society, admin. Hope Publishing Company, Carol Stream, IL 60188.

7. From "She Sits like a Bird," by John L. Bell and Graham Maule: CH 255, AHB 418, CH4 593. Copyright © 1988 by Wild Goose Resource Group, Iona Community, Scotland. G.I.A. Publications, Inc., exclusive North American agent.

8. From "Spirit," by James K. Manley: PH 319, CH 249, NCH 286, VU 375, BPR 399, TFWS 2120, ELW 396. Words and music copyright © 1978 by James K. Manley.

9. From "There's a Spirit in the Air," by Brian Wren: AMNS 515, HPS 326, RITL 380, UMH 192, PH 433, BH 393, BPW 300, RJS 329, CH 257, NCH 294, RSG 689, BPR 764, AHB 414, WP3 531, CH4 616. Copyright © 1969, 1995 by Hope Publishing Company for the U.S.A., Canada, Australia, and New Zealand, and by Stainer & Bell for all other territories.

10. "O Holy Spirit, Root of Life," by Jean Janzen, based on Hildegard von Bingen (1098–1179): CH 251, VU 379, BPR 391, TFWS 2121, ELW 399. Copyright © 1991 by Jean Janzen (admin. by Augsburg Fortress).

Chapter 4: Church

1. From "When the Church of Jesus Shuts Its Outer Door," by Fred Pratt Green: UMH 592, BH 396, BPW 614, CH 470. Copyright © 1969 by Hope Publishing Company, Carol Stream, IL 60188.

2. From "How Clear Is Our Vocation, Lord," by Fred Pratt Green: RITL 433, PH 419, HWB 541, VU 504, BPR 649, ELW 580. Copyright © 1982 by Hope Publishing Company, Carol Stream, IL 60188.

3. From "As a Chalice Cast of Gold," by Thomas H. Troeger: PH 336, CH 287, VU 505, BPR 593, AHB 476. Copyright © 1986 by Oxford University Press.

4. From "Christ Loves the Church," by Brian Wren: UMH 590. Copyright © 1986 by Hope Publishing Company for the U.S.A., Canada, Australia, and New Zealand, and by Stainer & Bell for all other territories.

5. From "Great God, Your Love Has Called Us Here" ("Lord God" in earlier hymnals), by Brian Wren: AMNS 489, HPS 500, RITL 503, UMH 579, PH 353, BPW 442, RJS 339, BPR 226, CH4 484, ELW 358. Copyright © 1975, 1995 by Hope Publishing Company for the U.S.A., Canada, Australia, and New Zealand, and by Stainer & Bell for all other territories.

6. From "Help Us Accept Each Other," by Fred Kaan: UMH 560, RJS 646, CH 487, NCH 388, RSG 838, BPR 632, AHB 648, WP3

656. See Romans 15:7 (*Revised English Bible*). Copyright © 1975 by Hope Publishing Company for the U.S.A. and Canada, and by Stainer & Bell for all other territories. The phrase "*know by heart . . . the table* of forgiveness" alludes, I think, to multiplication tables chanted and memorized ("Once two is two, two twos are four, three twos are six," etc.).

7. "Forgive Our Sins as We Forgive," by Rosamond Herklots (1905–87): AMNS 362, HPS 134, H82 674, PSH 266, UMH 390, PH 347, BPW 83, RJS 84, HWB 137, RSG 952, VU 364, BPR 751, AHB 635, WP3 754, CH4 486, ELW 605. Reproduced by permission of Oxford University Press.

8. From "When Love Is Found," by Brian Wren: UMH 643, CH 499, NCH 362, RSG 942, VU 489, BPR 600, AHB 654, WP3 745. Copyright © 1983 by Hope Publishing Company for the U.S.A., Canada, Australia, and New Zealand, and by Stainer & Bell for all other territories.

9. From "Brother, Sister, Let Me Serve You," by Richard Gillard (The Servant Song), emphasis mine (first line sometimes published as "Will You Let Me Be Your Servant?"): BPW 473, RJS 474, AA 8, RSG 788, BPR 635, AHB 650, TFWS 2222, CH4 694, ELW 659. Copyright ©1977 by Scripture in Song (admin. by Maranatha! Music).

10. From "We Are Your People," by Brian Wren: AMNS 519, RITL 419, PH 436, RJS 483, NCH 309, RSG 789, AHB 468, WP3 623. Copyright © 1975, 1995 by Hope Publishing Company for the U.S.A., Canada, Australia, and New Zealand, and by Stainer & Bell for all other territories.

11. "The Church of Christ in Every Age," by Fred Pratt Green: HPS 804, UMH 589, PH 421, BH 402, BPW 613, RJS 636, CH 475, NCH 306, RSG 803, VU 601, BPR 486, WP3 626, ELW 729. Copyright © 1971 by Hope Publishing Company, Carol Stream, IL 60188. American Lutherans asked for the changes. They omitted the "men/brotherhood" stanza and put the original second stanza last. These changes were the basis for the definitive version (which the author came to prefer), published in later hymnbooks.

Chapter 5: Worship

1. From "Here in This Place (Gather Us In)," by Marty Haugen: HWB 6, CH 284, RSG 850, AHB 474, TFWS 2236, WP3 665, CH4 623, ELW 532. Copyright © 1982 by G.I.A. Publications, Inc.

2. From "God Is Here!" by Fred Pratt Green: AMNS 464, HPS 653, PSH 516, UMH 660, PH 461, CH 280, NCH 70, RSG 844, VU 389, BPR 799, WP3 667, ELW 526. Copyright © 1979 by Hope Publishing Company, Carol Stream, IL 60188. See Matt. 18:20.

3. From "What Is This Place?" by Huub Oosterhuis: HWB 1, CH 289, RSG 892, WP3 709, ELW 524. Text and arrangement copyright © 1967, Gooi en Sticht, BV., Baarn, The Netherlands. Exclusive agent for English-language countries: O.C.P. Publications, 5536 N.E. Hassalo, Portland, OR 97213. Note the careful distinction between "*our* justice and *God's* peace."

4. From "Come and Find the Quiet Center," by Shirley Erena Murray: CH 575, VU 374, TFWS 2128, CH4 716. Copyright © 1992 by Hope Publishing Company, Carol Stream, IL 60188.

5. From "As a Chalice Cast of Gold," by Thomas H. Troeger: PH 336, CH 287, VU 505, BPR 593, AHB 476. See also chap. 4, n. 3. Copyright © 1986 by Oxford University Press.

6. From "Lord, Whose Love in Humble Service," by Albert F. Bayly (1901–84): H82 610, PSH 603, UMH 581, PH 427, HWB 369, CH 461, RSG 793, BPR 722, WP3 630, ELW 712. Copyright © 1988 by Oxford University Press.

7. From "O Praise the Gracious Power," by Thomas H. Troeger: PH 471, BH 226, HWB 111, NCH 54, VU 397, ELW 651. Copyright © 1986 by Oxford University Press.

8. From "Child of Blessing, Child of Promise," by Ronald S. Cole-Turner: UMH 611, PH 498, HWB 620, AA 11, NCH 325, VU 444, BPR 521, CH4 633. Copyright ©1981 by Ronald S. Cole-Turner.

9. From "Will You Come and Follow Me" (The Summons), by John Bell and Graham Maule: BPW 363, RJS 558, RSG 811, VU 567, BPR 634, TFWS 2130, CH4 533, ELW 798. Copyright © 1987 by Wild Goose Resource Group, Iona Community, Scotland. G.I.A. Publications, Inc, exclusive North American agent.

10. From "Lord, When You Came to the Seashore" (Pescador de Hombres): UMH 344, PH 377, HWB 229, CH 342, NCH 173, RSG 817, VU 563, ELW 817. Spanish text and music copyright © 1979 by Cesáreo Gabaráin; published by O.C.P. Publications, 5536 N.E. Hassalo, Portland, OR 97213. English text copyright © 1982 by Willard F. Jabusch (admin. by O.C.P. Publications).

11. From "An Upper Room Did Our Lord Prepare," by Fred Pratt Green: AMNS 434, HPS 594, RITL 568, PH 94, RJS 438, VU 139, BPR 224, AHB 536. Copyright © 1974 by Hope Publishing Company, Carol Stream, IL 60188.

12. From "Let Us Talents and Tongues Employ," by Fred Kaan: AMNS 481, PH 514, CH 422, NCH 347, VU 468, BPR 563, AHB 537, CH4 673, ELW 674. Emphasis mine. Copyright © 1975 by Hope Publishing Company, Carol Stream, IL 60188.

13. From "I Come with Joy," by Brian Wren: AMNS 473, HPS 610, RITL 534, H82 304, PSH 311, UMH 617, PH 507, BH 371, BPW 437, RJS 447, HWB 459, CH 420, NCH 349, RSG 854, VU 477, BPR 530, AHB 533, WP3 726, CH4 656, ELW 482. Copyright © 1969, 1982, 1994 by Hope Publishing Company for the U.S.A.,

Canada, Australia, and New Zealand, and by Stainer & Bell for all other territories. I am using the 1994 revision.

14. From "You Satisfy the Hungry Heart" (Gift of Finest Wheat), by Omer Westendorf: PSH 300, UMH 629, PH 521, CH 429, RSG 912, BPR 538, AHB 539, CH4 671, ELW 484. Copyright © 1977 by the Archdiocese of Philadelphia.

15. Fom "One Bread, One Body," John B. Foley, S.J.: UMH 620, CH 393, RSG 915, VU 467, BPR 540, CH4 665, ELW 496. Copyright © 1978 by John B. Foley, SJ; admin. O.C.P. Publications, 5536 N.E. Hassalo, Portland, OR 97213.

16. From "Now the Silence," by Jaroslav Vajda: H82 333, UMH 619, HWB 462, CH 415, VU 475, BPR 562. BPR 562 also prints Vajda's equally original "Then." Carl Schalk's tune NOW is indispensable for both texts and was composed in consultation with their author. Both hymns are copyright © 1969 by Hope Publishing Company, Carol Stream, IL 60188.

17. "Jesu, Jesu," by Tom Colvin: HPS 145, H82 602, PSH 601, UMH 432, PH 367, BH 501, BPW 606, RJS 648, CH 600, RSG 564, WP3 431, ELW 708. Copyright © 1969 by Hope Publishing Company, Carol Stream, IL 60188.

18. From "O Christ, the Healer," by Fred Pratt Green: HPS 395, UMH 265, PH 380, HWB 379, CH 503, NCH 175, AHB 638, WP3 747, CH4 717, ELW 610. Copyright © 1969 by Hope Publishing Company, Carol Stream, IL 60188.

19. From "When Memory Fades and Recognition Falters," by Mary Louise Bringle: CH4 701, ELW 792. Copyright © 2002 by G.I.A. Publications, Inc.

20. From "Christ's Is the World in Which We Move" (A Touching Place), by John Bell and Graham Maule: BPR 758, AHB 677, CH4 724. Copyright © 1989 byWild Goose Resource Group, Iona Community, Scotland. G.I.A. Publications, Inc., exclusive North American agent.

21. From "Lord, Whose Love in Humble Service," by Albert Bayly. See note 7, above.

22. From"Now Let Us from This Table Rise," by Fred Kaan: AMNS 403, HPS 619, UMH 634, BPW 451, RJS 463, VU 483, BPR 556, AHB 530, WP3 625, CH4 675. Copyright © 1968 by Hope Publishing Company for the U.S.A. and Canada, and by Stainer & Bell for all other territories.

Chapter 6: Witness

1. The act of anointing with oil.

2. From "Lord, You Give the Great Commission," by Jeffery Rowthorn: PSH 523, UMH 584, PH 429, RJS 580, CH 459, RSG 607, VU 512, BPR 778, WP3 470, ELW 579. Copyright © 1978 by Hope Publishing Company, Carol Stream, IL 60188.

3. From "We All Are One in Mission," by Rusty Edwards: H82 673, PH 435, TFWS 2243, ELW 576. Copyright © 1986 by Hope Publishing Company, Carol Stream, IL 60188.

4. From "Arise, Your Light Has Come," by Ruth Duck: RITL 418, PH 411, BH 83, NCH 164, VU 79, BPR 712, ELW 314. Copyright © 1992 by G.I.A. Publications, Inc..

5. From "O God of Every Nation," by William Watkins Reid Jr.: H82 607, PSH 606, UMH 435, PH 289, CH 680, VU 677, AHB 621, WP3 650, ELW 713. Copyright © 1958 renewed 1986 by The Hymn Society in the U.S. and Canada (admin. Hope Publishing Co., Carol Stream, IL 60188).

6. From "We Cannot Own the Sunlit Sky," by Ruth Duck: CH 684, NCH 563, BPR 717, MV 143. Copyright © 1992 by G.I.A. Publications, Inc.

7. From "O for a World," by Miriam Therese Winter: PH 386, CH 683, NCH 575, VU 697, BPR 730. Copyright © 1987 by Medical Mission Sisters.

8. From "For the Healing of the Nations," by Fred Kaan: AMNS 361, HPS 402, UMH 428, BPW 621, RJS 620, HWB 367, CH 668, NCH 576, RSG 823, WP3 643, CH4 706. Copyright © 1968 by Hope Publishing Company, Carol Stream, IL 60188.

9. From "Now Join We to Praise the Creator," by Fred Kaan: AMNS 500, HPS 348, BPW 612, RJS 89, RSG 827, WP3 647. Emphases mine. Copyright © 1989 by Hope Publishing Company for the U.S.A., Canada, Australia, and New Zealand, and by Stainer & Bell for all other territories.

10. "O God, We Bear the Imprint of Your Face," by Shirley Erena Murray: PH 385, AA 106, CH 681, NCH 585, CH4 254. Copyright © 1987 by Hope Publishing Company, Carol Stream, IL 60188. This hymn needs a careful choice of tune. To my ear, Orlando Gibbons's SONG 1 (as in *The Presbyterian Hymnal,* U.S.A.) has rich harmonies that are at odds with the stark ending—though it works well if sung unaccompanied on the melody line. Dan Damon's RAUMATI BEACH (*Chalice Hymnal,* U.S.A.) is a better fit, and its equal note values allow for the variations in the text's meaning and mood. Similarly, Geoffrey Laycock's tune HARVEST (*Rejoice and Sing,* U.K.) accommodates the changing moods of Fred Kaan's "Now Join We, to Praise the Creator." See note 9.

11. From "Jesus Christ Is Waiting," by John Bell and Graham Maule: BPW 534, VU 117, AHB 665, CH4 360. Copyright © 1988 by Wild Goose Resource Group, Iona Community, Scotland. G.I.A. Publications, Inc, exclusive North American agent.

12. "Go Down, Moses!" is in the public domain. "What Does the Lord Require?" is a widely published hymn by Albert F. Bayly: AMNS 432, HPS 414, RITL 176, H82 605, PSH 293, UMH 441, PH 405, HWB 409, CH 659, RSG 785, BPR 710, AHB 618, WP3 624. Copy-

right © 1988 by Oxford University Press. Some hymnals tone it down by eliminating its economic dimension ("Leaders in wealth and trade . . .").

13. From "When the Poor Ones," by José Antonio Olivar (trans. Martin A. Seltz): UMH 434, PH 407, VU 702, BPR 762, CH4 258, ELW 725. Copyright © 1971 by J. A. Olivar, Miguel Manzano, and San Pablo Internacional–SSP. Sole U.S. agent and publisher, O.C.P. Publications, Inc., 5536 N.E. Hassalo, Portland, OR 97213.

14. From "Put Peace into Each Other's Hands," by Fred Kaan: BPW 638, RJS 635, BPR 560, CH4 659, MV 173. Copyright © 1989 by Hope Publishing Company, Carol Stream, IL 60188.

15. "O Day of Peace!" by Carl P. Daw Jr.: UMH 729, PH 450, HWB 408, CH 711, VU 682, BPR 732, WP3 654, ELW 711. Copyright © 1982 by Hope Publishing Company, Carol Stream, IL 60188.

16. From "God, Who Stretched the Spangled Heavens," by Catherine Cameron: RITL 29, H82 580, UMH 150, PH 268, BH 47, RJS 86, RSG 819, BPR 305, AHB 163, WP3 648, ELW 771. Copyright © 1967 by Hope Publishing Company, Carol Stream, IL 60188.

17. From "O Lord of Every Shining Constellation," by Albert F. Bayly: AMNS 411, RITL 31, PH 297, BPW 130, CH 55, BPR 302, AHB 157, CH4 246. Copyright © 1988 by Oxford University Press.

18. "Touch the Earth Lightly," by Shirley Murray: AA 143, CH 693, NCH 569, VU 307, AHB 668, CH4 243, ELW 739. Copyright © 1992 by Hope Publishing Company, Carol Stream, IL 60188.

19. Some still call them "weak" or "feminine" endings, but let them simmer in their sexism.

20. From "Give to Me, Lord, a Thankful Heart," by Thomas Caryl Micklem (1925–2003): HPS 548, RITL 462, PH 351, BPW 531, RJS 497, VU 513. Copyright © 1975 by Ruth Micklem.

21. From "How Clear Is Our Vocation, Lord," by Fred Pratt Green: RITL 433, PH 419, HWB 541, VU 504, BPR 649, ELW 580. Copyright © 1982 by Hope Publishing Company, Carol Stream, IL 60188.

22. From "Here I Am, Lord," by Daniel Schutte: UMH 593, PH 525, HWB 395, CH 452, RSG 802, VU 509, BPR 592, AHB 658, CH4 251, ELW 574. Text and music copyright © 1981 by O.C.P. Publications, Inc., 5536 N.E. Hassalo, Portland OR 97213. Besides Isa. 6:8, Schutte's hymn also echoes Isa. 25:6; 35:6; and 41:17; and Ezek. 11:19.

Chapter 7: Praise

1. See Carlton R. Young, *Companion to the United Methodist Hymnal* (Nashville: Abingdon Press, 1993), 636–37. Web searches turn up varied accounts of what Olivers did.

2. "You Are Before Me, Lord, You Are Behind," by Ian Pitt-Watson (1923–95): RITL 138, PH 248, RJS 731, VU 862, BPR 101, AHB 87, CH4 96. Copyright © 1973 by the Estate of Ian Pitt-Watson.

3. "The Care the Eagle Gives Her Young," by R. Deane Postlethwaite (1925–80): UMH 118, HWB 590, CH 76, NCH 468, VU 269. Copyright © 1980 by Marjean Postlethwaite. I don't know the ornithological basis of Deut. 32:11.

4. From "Bring Many Names," by Brian Wren: CH 10, NCH 11, VU 268, BPR 310, AHB 182, TFWS 2047, and CH4 134. Copyright © 1989 by Hope Publishing Company for the U.S.A., Canada, Australia, and New Zealand, and by Stainer & Bell for all other territories. Because femaleness and maleness are created jointly in the image and likeness of God (Gen. 1:27), both genders can reveal the divine. Reversing gender stereotypes makes visible the women whose genius can "set equations," and gives a picture of fatherhood in tune with the Abba to whom Jesus prayed (Matt. 6:26 and 7:11). Different stages in our life cycle can give glimpses of God: as a white-haired "ancient one" (Dan. 7:9), as divinity embodied in an infant and in passion analogous to youthful intolerance of "falsehood and unkindness" (see, e.g., Isa. 2:13–17; Amos 5:21–24).

5. From "God of the Sparrow," by Jaroslav Vajda: UMH 122, PH 272, CH 70, NCH 32, VU 229, BPR 307, ELW 740. Copyright © 1983 by Concordia Publishing House. Vajda's Scripture sources appear to be King James Version ("Authorized Version" in U.K.). The less obvious include "sparrow" (Matt. 10:29–31); whale (Gen. 1:21—NRSV has "sea monster"); "earthquake" (e.g., 1 Kgs. 19:11; Amos 1:1; Matt. 27:54; Rev. 6:12; 8:6); "storm" (Job 21:18 and Ps. 83:15—NRSV has "tempest"); trumpet blast (several in Rev., chaps. 9–11); "neighbor" and "foe" (Matt. 5:43–44); "pruning hook" (Isa. 2:4); and "prodigal" (Luke 5:11–24—still often called the parable of the Prodigal [spendthrift] Son).

6. "Early theologians speak as if Father, Son, and Spirit are labels rather than images, claiming that God comes with the biblical name Father . . . not that God acts like a father and thus acquires the title metaphorically," Gail Ramshaw, *God beyond Gender* (Minneapolis: Fortress Press, 1995), 80.

7. From "Creating God, Your Fingers Trace," by Jeffery Rowthorn: PSH 605, UMH 109, PH 134, RJS 56, HWB 325, CH 335, NCH 462, RSG 711, BPR 288, ELW 684. Copyright © 1979 by The Hymn Society in the U.S. and Canada (admin. Hope Publishing Company, Carol Stream, IL 60188).

8. "Source and Sovereign, Rock and Cloud," by Thomas H. Troeger: UMH 113, CH 12, CH4 133. Copyright © 1986 by Oxford University Press.

9. From "Womb of Life, and Source of Being," by Ruth Duck: CH 14, NCH 274, TFWS 2046, CH4 118. Copyright © 1992 by G.I.A. Publications, Inc.

10. From "God the Spirit, Guide and Guardian," by Carl P. Daw Jr: UMH 653, PH 523, HWB 632, CH 450, NCH 355, VU 514, BPR 589.

Copyright © 1989 by Hope Publishing Company, Carol Stream, IL 60188.

11. "Mothering God, You Gave Me Birth," by Jean Janzen: HWB 482, CH 83, NCH 46, VU 320, BPR 312, TFWS 2050, CH4 117, ELW 735. Copyright © 1991 by Jean Janzen, admin. Augsburg Fortress.

12. From "By Gracious Powers," by Dietrich Bonhoeffer, trans. Fred Pratt Green: RITL 55, H82 695, UMH 517, PH 342, BPW 117, RJS 486, HWB 552, NCH 413, BPR 658, WP3 577, ELW 626. Translation copyright © 1974 by Hope Publishing Company, Carol Stream, IL 60188.

13. From "Lord of the Living," by Fred Kaan: HPS 654, PH 529, VU 492, BPR 603, AHB 637, WP3 739. Copyright © 1968 by Hope Publishing Company for the U.S.A. and Canada, and by Stainer & Bell for all other territories.

14. "Why Has God Forsaken Me?" by William L. Wallace: PH 406, HWB 246, VU 154, TFWS 2110, CH4 388. Copyright © 1981 by Selah Publications.

15. From "This Is a Day of New Beginnings," by Brian Wren: UMH 383, BH 370, HWB 640, CH 518, NCH 417, AHB 653, WP3 661, CH4 526. Copyright © 1978 by Hope Publishing Company for the U.S.A., Canada, Australia, and New Zealand, and by Stainer & Bell for all other territories.

16. From "One More Step along the World I Go," by Sydney Carter: HPS 746, BPW 356, RJS 549, VU 639, BPR 641, CH4 530. Copyright © 1971 by Stainer & Bell Ltd. (admin. in North America by Hope Publishing Company, Carol Stream, IL 60188).

17. From "Then the Glory," by Jaroslav Vajda: BPR 562. Copyright © 1969 by Hope Publishing Company, Carol Stream, IL 60188.

18. "In the Bulb There Is a Flower" (Hymn of Promise, by Natalie Sleeth: UMH 707, HWB 614, CH 638, NCH 433, VU 703, BPR 674, CH4 727. Copyright © 1986 by Hope Publishing Company, Carol Stream, IL 60188.

19. "When in Our Music God Is Glorified," by Fred Pratt Green: HPS 388, RITL 508, UMH 68, PH 264, BH 435, RJS 414, HWB 44, CH 7, NCH 561, RSG 665, VU 533, BPR 439, WP3 549, CH4 203, ELW 851. Copyright © 1972 by Hope Publishing Company, Carol Stream, IL 60188.

Chapter 8: Treasure

1. Originally "quickened."

Index of Authors

Further Reading

For others and titles out of print, ask the publishers or try a name search online, or Amazon online.

Major publishers' contact information follows this list.

Albert Bayly

    Rejoice, O People: Hymns and Poems (Chipping Norton, U.K.: Nigel Lynn and the Hymn Society of Great Britain and Ireland, 2004)

John L. Bell and Graham Maule

    Heaven Shall Not Wait—Wild Goose Songs, Vol. 1: *Songs of Creation, Incarnation, and the Life of Jesus* (G.I.A. Publications, 1989)

    Wild Goose Songs, Vol. 2: *Passion, Resurrection, and Holy Spirit* (G.I.A. Publications, 1988)

    When Grief Is Raw: Songs for Times of Sorrow and Bereavement (G.I.A. Publications, 1997)

    Love and Anger: Songs of Lively Faith and Social Justice (G.I.A. Publications, 1997)

Mary Louise Bringle

    Joy and Wonder, Love and Longing: 75 Hymn Texts (G.I.A. Publications, 2002)

    In Wind and Wonder: 75 Hymn Texts (G.I.A. Publications, 2007)

Dan Damon

    *Faith Will Sing: 24 New Hymns (*Hope Publishing Company, 1993)

    The Sound of Welcome: 25 New Hymns (Hope Publishing Company, 1998)

    *To the Thirsty World: New Hymns for a New Day (*Nashville: Abingdon Press, 2002)

    Fields of Mercy: 33 New Hymns and Chants (Hope Publishing Company, 2007)

Carl P. Daw Jr.
>   *A Year of Grace: Collected Hymns* (Hope Publishing Company, 1992)
>   *New Psalms and Hymns and Spiritual Songs* (Hope Publishing Company,
>   1996)

Ruth Duck
>   *Dancing in the Universe: Hymns and Songs* (G.I.A. Publications, 1992)
>   *Circles of Care: Hymns and Songs* (Cleveland: The Pilgrim Press. 1998)
>   *Welcome God's Tomorrow: 35 Hymn Texts* (G.I.A. Publications, 2005)

Timothy Dudley-Smith
>   *A House of Praise: Collected Hymns, 1961–2001* (Oxford University Press
>   and Hope Publishing Company, 2003)

Sylvia G. Dunstan
>   *In Search of Hope and Grace* (G.I.A. Publications, 1991)
>   *Where the Promise Shines* (G.I.A. Publications, 1995)

Rusty Edwards
>   *The Yes of the Heart* (Hope Publishing Company, 1992)

Fred Pratt Green
>   *The Hymns and Ballads of Fred Pratt Green* (Hope Publishing Company,
>   1982)
>   *Later Hymns and Ballads and Fifty Poems* (Hope Publishing Company and
>   Stainer & Bell, U.S.A. and U.K., 1989)

Fred Kaan
>   *The Only Earth We Know: Hymn Texts* (Stainer & Bell and Hope Publishing
>   Company, 1992)

Shirley Murray
>   *In Every Corner Sing: 80 Hymns* (Hope Publishing Company, 1992)
>   *Every Day in Your Spirit* (Hope Publishing Company, 1996)
>   *Faith Makes the Song* (Hope Publishing Company, 2003)
>   *Touch the Earth Lightly* (Hope Publishing Company, 2008)

Jeffery Rowthorn
>   *Singing Songs of Expectation: Songs for Today's Pilgrims* (Hope Publishing
>   Company, 2008)

Thomas H. Troeger
>   *Borrowed Light: Hymn Texts, Prayers and Poems* (New York and Oxford:
>   Oxford University Press, 1994)

Jaroslav Vajda
  Now the Joyful Celebration (St. Louis: Morningstar Publications, 1987)
  So Much to Sing About (St. Louis: Morningstar Publications, 1991)

Brian Wren
  *Piece Together Praise: A Theological Journey—Poems and Collected
  Hymns Thematically Arranged* (Texts of Wren hymns to 1996, with first-
  line index in back that includes tune sources (Stainer & Bell and Hope
  Publishing Company, 1996)
  Visions and Revisions: 33 New Hymns and Seven Reissues (Hope Publishing
  Company, 1998)
  Christ Our Hope: 33 New Hymns and Six Reissues (Hope Publishing Com-
  pany, 2004)
  Love's Open Door: Hymns and Songs (2004–2008) (Hope Publishing Com-
  pany, 2009)

Major Hymn Publishers

G.I.A. Publications, 7404 S. Mason Ave., Chicago IL 60638-3438, U.S.A.
  http://www.giamusic.com/

Hope Publishing Company, 380 South Main Place, Carol Stream IL 60188,
U.S.A.
  http://www.hopepublishing.com

Morningstar Music, St. Louis, U.S.A.
  http://www.morningstarmusic.com/

Oxford University Press—U.K. and Europe
  http://www.oup.co.U.K./music/

Oxford University Press—U.S.A.
  http://www.oup.com/us/corporate/publishingprograms/music/

Stainer & Bell Ltd, PO Box 110, Victoria House, 23 Gruneisen Road, London,
England N3 1DZ
  http://www.stainer.co.U.K./

Hymn Societies—Conferences, Publications, and Interest Networks

Hymn Society in the U.S. and Canada
  http://www.hymnsociety.org

142 Further Reading

The Hymn Society of Great Britain and Ireland
http://www.hymnsocietygbi.org.U.K./

International Fellowship for Research in Hymnology
(International Arbeitsgemeinschaft für Hymnologie)
(Cercle international d'études hymnologiques)
http://www.iah.unibe.ch/